Engl 6..
1 50

A TREATISE ON THE NOVEL

A TREATISE
ON THE NOVEL

by

ROBERT LIDDELL

Il y a autre chose à faire d'une belle
œuvre que de la copier, c'est de rivaliser
avec elle. Ce n'est pas ses résultats qu'elle
nous enseigne, ce sont ses moyens.

CLAUDEL: *Le Soulier de Satin*,
deuxième journée, sc. v

JONATHAN CAPE
THIRTY BEDFORD SQUARE
LONDON

FIRST PUBLISHED SEPTEMBER 1947
SECOND IMPRESSION 1949

PRINTED IN GREAT BRITAIN IN THE CITY OF OXFORD
AT THE ALDEN PRESS
BOUND BY A. W. BAIN & CO. LTD., LONDON

CONTENTS

CONTENTS

6

CONTENTS

ACKNOWLEDGEMENTS

I wish to thank Mr. P. H. Newby for reading the manuscript of this book, and for making several valuable suggestions.

Thanks are also due to Mr. T. S. Eliot and Messrs. Faber & Faber for permission to use extracts from *Second Thoughts on Humanism*, to the executors of Henry James for permission to quote from *The Art of the Novel*, to Librairie Gallimard for permission to quote from the works of Marcel Proust, and to Miss I. Compton-Burnett for permission to use illustrative passages from her works.

NOTES TO CHAPTERS

For the translations from the French I am generally responsible. Those from *Madame Bovary*, however, are taken from the *Everyman* translation. The edition of Flaubert's letters used is that of Bibliothèque-Charpentier (Paris 1920).

A TREATISE ON THE NOVEL

CHAPTER I

AN APPROACH TO THE CRITICISM OF FICTION

§1 THE DIGNITY OF THE NOVEL

THE Novel as a literary form has still a flavour of newness. It is true that it can trace its descent from Longus, Heliodorus and Petronius, and from medieval prose romances; it is true, but not very interesting, and more learning than thought has been employed to trace this descent, which is no uncommon thing in Genealogy. In a family that has in modern times produced great men, *they* are what we care about; we are impatient with long accounts of their remoter ancestors, though they must of course have had ancestors. In the same way prose fiction before the eighteenth century can only matter to us as scholars, not as critics or general readers.

When we remember what the romances of his time were like, we are not indignant with Bossuet for praising Henriette d'Angleterre, in his funeral oration upon her, because she did not care for novels. 'Our admirable princess studied the duties of those whose lives make up history; there she insensibly lost the taste for romances and for their insipid heroes, and, anxious to form herself upon truth, she despised those cold and dangerous fictions.'

Even in our own times the Novel is sometimes still attacked; but though we can readily pardon Bossuet, it is not so easy to pardon those who attack a form that has been used by Jane Austen, by Stendhal, by Tolstoy, by Flaubert, by Henry James and by Proust. Attacks upon the Novel as a form have adversely influenced both novelists and critics, many of whose worst errors can directly be traced to a low view of this form of art.

The case put forward against the novel by Mr. Montgomery

Belgion may be examined, although his book has perhaps been forgotten. His argument should be answered in case it is ever put forward again by anyone else.

Mr. Belgion says that there is no such thing as a creative artist; and, since a novelist is not a creative artist, there is only one thing he can be, a propagandist for his own particular view of life, and an irresponsible propagandist at that. The title of creative artist is denied to the novelist because 'to create' means 'to bring into existence out of nothing': characters in fiction have never been made out of nothing, but always out of some shreds of experience; and they never come into existence — we cannot take them by the hand.[1]

The answer is simple and obvious. We regard ourselves and our neighbours as individually created beings, although none of *us* was made out of nothing. And there is more than one way of existing: Wisdom and Virtue exist, although you cannot take either of them by the hand. Therefore although Falstaff or Mrs. Gamp may not belong to the same order of being as Napoleon, it is nevertheless not unreasonable to say that they exist, and that they have been created by their authors.

But even allowing the novelist to be a creative artist, some people think his art a very inferior one. Several novelists are unfortunately of this opinion. 'Oh dear, the novel tells a story,' says Mr. Forster regretfully,[2] and clearly wishes that it did not. Mr. Forster at least dwells with more complacency on the fact that the novel depicts character, but even that Mr. Aldous Huxley thinks a trivial thing to do. A character of his reflects (with his apparent approval) on 'the wearisomeness to an adult mind, of all those merely descriptive plays and novels which critics expected one to admire. All the innumerable, interminable anecdotes and romances and character-studies, but no general theory of anecdotes, no explanatory hypothesis of romance or character. Just a huge collection of facts about lust and greed, fear and ambition, duty and affection; just facts and imaginary facts at that, with no co-ordinating philosophy superior to common sense and the local system of conventions, no principle of arrangement more rational than simple aesthetic expediency.'³

It is very shocking to find that a novelist thinks facts about Human Nature so wearisome, when they should be his stock-in-trade. It is worse that he wishes for any arrangement of those facts other than 'simple aesthetic expediency' — what principle for an artist could be more rational? And his contempt for the imagination does not make things any better. We shall see, in a subsequent chapter, that for a novelist no philosophy is superior to common sense.

If we turn away from Mr. Huxley to a novelist of creative genius, who respected and loved her art, to Jane Austen, we shall find a character whom she wishes to ridicule expressing himself in terms very similar to those of Mr. Huxley's would-be intelligent character.

Sir Edward Denham in *Sanditon*, the fragment left unfinished by Miss Austen at her death, makes this boast: 'I am no indiscriminate Novel-Reader. The mere trash of the common Circulating-Library, I hold in the highest contempt. You will never hear me advocating those puerile Emanations which detail nothing but discordant Principles incapable of Amalgamation, or those vapid tissues of ordinary Occurrences from which no useful Deductions can be drawn. In vain may we put them into a literary Alembic; we distil nothing which can add to Science.'

Sir Edward's pomposity is a prophetic parody of that of Mr. Huxley and of all others who are not content that a novel should be a novel, but want it to be something else as well — as if to be a good novel were not enough. And it is just that Mr. Huxley should be rebuked out of the mouth of Miss Austen, for in depreciating the Novel, and thereby fouling his own nest, he is doing precisely the thing that she had condemned in a famous passage in *Northanger Abbey*.

'I will not adopt that ungenerous and impolitic custom, so common with novel writers, of degrading, by their contemptuous censure, the very performance to the number of which they are themselves adding; joining with their greatest enemies in bestowing the harshest epithets on such works, and scarcely ever permitting them to be read by their own heroine, who, if she accidentally take up a novel, is sure to turn over its insipid pages with disgust ... There seems almost a general wish of decrying the capacity and undervaluing the labour of the novelist, and of slighting the performances which have only genius, wit, and taste to recommend them. "And what are you reading, Miss — ?" "Oh, it is only a novel," replies the young lady; while she lays down her book with affected indifference or momentary shame. It is only *Cecilia*, or *Camilla*, or *Belinda*, or in short, only some work in which the most thorough knowledge of human nature, the happiest delineation of its varieties, the liveliest effusions of wit and humour are conveyed to the world in the best chosen language.'

There has not yet been made a more eloquent defence of the novel. No further apology is needed for asserting the dignity of that literary form which enables 'the most thorough knowledge of human nature, the happiest delineation of its varieties, the liveliest effusions of wit and humour' to be 'conveyed to the world in the best chosen language'.

§2 THE NOVEL, AND THE HERITAGE OF DRAMA

Saintsbury, the genealogist of the Novel, insisted on its ancient history, for its history was identical with that of the Romance, whether in prose or verse. He argued that it was unhistorical, and otherwise unexampled, for a literary genre to appear for the first time in the eighteenth century — when epic, tragedy, comedy, the essay and the epigram can all be traced back to the literatures of Greece and Rome. Moreover, he argued, if we are to call the Romance and the Novel different genres before the eighteenth century, then we must logically maintain this difference during and after the eighteenth century — which it would be difficult to do. Lastly he said that it was artificial to contrast the Romance, or story of incident, with the Novel, or story of character and motive — since every story with people in it is potentially a novel.

Without directly contesting Saintsbury's arguments, one may differ from him so completely in values that their force vanishes. Suppose that we grant that it is unhistorical to say that the first novel appeared about two hundred years ago, and that the literary genre must have a longer history — yet it is possible to maintain that a qualitative change occurred at some point, so great that in order to study the Novel after this development we get little help from examples of what (one may grant) was the same literary form before the development.

There are parallels enough for a change of this sort — in literature one may quote the development of Greek drama during the lifetime of Aeschylus, or of English drama during the lifetime of Marlowe. Outside literature, we know that music and wine were so much poorer and thinner things to the Ancient World than they are to-day, as hardly to be recognizable.

The danger of insisting too much on the long history of the Novel, the chief fault to be found with those many-volumed histories of fiction in which Richardson comes nearly half-way, is that we are thereby blinded to the important heritage which the modern novel has received — not from earlier novelists, but from the Drama. The relation between the Novel and the Drama should be understood, as a preliminary to criticism. The history of the Drama is the pre-history of the Novel.

It may be said, shortly and dogmatically, but with infinitely more truth than such statements in literary history are commonly made, that the English theatre died in 1700 — a glorious death, after its most brilliant comedy, *The Way of the World* — and that the English novel was born, with *Pamela*, in 1740. There must be some connection between these two events, and of course there is. Poetry, having separated from Drama, has led an independent life ever since, for the most part little concerned with the representation of character in action. As for the representation of character in action — here the Novel succeeded to the Play, and minds that in other ages would have been devoted to the Drama have been devoted to fiction. We may attribute much of the tedium of pre-Richardsonian fiction to the fact that it was the work of essentially uncreative minds, more creative minds being in the service of the stage. On the other hand, if the entire Drama of the western world written in the last two hundred years were to be lost, there would be very few master-pieces to grieve for — and among those few there would not be any English plays.

Although the Novel is the rightful heir to the Drama, and in England (at least) has been the natural prose form for a creative mind to adopt since the time of Richardson, this aspect of the situation was far from obvious to the earlier novelists, and has perhaps not yet been fully accepted. The English drama (with some interruptions) had had a life of such incomparable brilliance for a hundred and ten years, that it must have been hard in the eighteenth century to think of it as extinct or dormant. Fielding, an unsuccessful dramatist, thought that in *Joseph Andrews* he was attempting a different art, that of Comic Epic. His attitude to character and plot was therefore, deliberately, epic rather than dramatic. He was far too conscious an artist, far too well drilled in Aristotle, to be content with a plot that did not exhibit unity of action to some extent, though he allowed himself an epic poet's liberties in the introduction of episodes. Such liberties were extended by Smollett, and his admirer Dickens to the licence of the novel of 'the English school' — a 'prose romance' or 'comic epic' of a purely episodic nature, kept together only by unity of hero, and called by the hero's name: such as *The Adventures of Roderick Random* or *The Life and Adventures of Nicholas Nickleby*.

Until George Eliot restored Unity of Action as a principle, it was the exception in the English novel — to be found in the novels of Jane Austen, in *Vanity Fair* and *Esmond*, in *Wuthering Heights*, and in such uncharacteristic work of Scott and Dickens as *The Bride of Lammermoor* and *Great Expectations*. And only Jane Austen and Emily Brontë are insistent the whole time that their characters shall unremittingly contribute to the plot.

It was perhaps Henry James, another unsuccessful dramatist, who was the first to show us deliberately, in *The Awkward Age*, that the Novel could do everything that the Drama can — later, in *The Ambassadors*, he showed us how much it could do that the Drama cannot. Nevertheless a critic like Mr. Forster is still so much under the spell of the great name of Drama that he can write of 'a novel which ought to have been a play'[4] — though he does not tell us why any novel ought to have been a play, or what it would gain. It is hard to see what function prose Drama now retains that cannot be better performed by the Cinema or the Novel — and hard, with the best will in the world, to regard modern verse Drama as more than a picturesque revival of an ancient custom.

Aristotle is still worked far too hard as a literary critic, and it is little more than a waste of time to apply his generalizations about a literature with which he was thoroughly familiar, to a literature which he could not have foreseen. Nevertheless, without being pedantic about Unity of Action, without having what Jane Austen called 'starched notions' about the Novel, and while admitting a degree of legitimate difference in taste, it is reasonable to claim that such structurally perfect novels as *Emma*, *Madame Bovary* and *The Ambassadors*, whose underlying principle is dramatic rather than epic, belong to a higher artistic order than the more rambling of the Waverley novels or *Martin Chuzzlewit*.

With the rest of the heritage of the Drama, the Novel came into its position as the dominant literary form. The dangers to a literary form of dominance have been well set out by Mr. C. S. Lewis. 'Its characteristics are formalized. A stereotyped monotony unnoticed by contemporaries but cruelly apparent to posterity, begins to invade it . . . In the second place, a dominant form tends to attract to itself writers whose talents would have fitted them much better for work of some other kind . . . And thirdly — which is most disastrous — a dominant form attracts to itself those who ought not to have written at all;

it becomes a kind of trap or drain towards which bad work moves by a certain "kindly enclyning". Youthful vanity and dullness, determined to write, will almost certainly write in the dominant form of their epoch.'[5]

With these characteristics of a dominant form, the criticism of fiction must be equipped to deal.

§3 CATEGORIES OF THE NOVEL

The contemporary novel falls roughly into two main categories, each of which may be sub-divided into two sub-categories. (This classification is influenced by, though not directly derived from, *Fiction and the Reading Public* by Q. D. Leavis, a work which professes to be anthropological rather than critical, and therefore requires a different system of arrangement.)

I. Novels which call for serious literary criticism.

(*a*) Good novels.

Though the critic will refuse to establish any sort of examination-order of novelists, or to give marks to their work, yet he may properly speak of e.g. 'great novels', and of 'minor classics'. The terms have been abused, but they still have meaning; it is part of the critic's duty to restore value to such distinctions.

(*b*) Novels which might have been good.

The writers had minds of the necessary sensibility; but for some reason the books are bad, or uneven, or technical failures.

In this class may be placed the failures of good novelists, and books by writers 'whose talents would have fitted them much better for work of some other kind'.

II. Novels which are beneath serious criticism.

(*a*) 'Middlebrow'.

(*b*) 'Lowbrow'.

From the point of view of literature it is of course not worth distinguishing between the two main categories of fiction regarded as beneath criticism. As Dr. Johnson would say, it is like establishing the precedence between a flea and a louse. But entomology may distinguish properly between a flea and a louse though it is not the business of etiquette to do so. From her own sociological or anthropological point of view Mrs. Leavis's distinction between what she calls 'middlebrow' and 'lowbrow' work is of value.[6] Her analysis ought to be used more than it is by reviewers, who seldom have the material offered to them upon which serious critical work can be done. Moreover, it is certainly the duty of reviewers to indicate those middlebrow writers who, in her words: 'are making for enlightenment and, in a confused way, for more desirable (but not finer) feeling . . . doing a very necessary work in a society of dwellers on a rising series of plateaux, the work of keeping the lower levels posted with news of what is stirring higher up.'[7]

It would also be worth while to point out such 'middlebrow' fiction as presents interest on account of its subject-matter, or its technical skill in managing some special device, or meeting some specific difficulty. Such reasons may make ephemeral work worth reading for some years after its publication; they do not confer on it the title of literature, which distinguishes only such reading-matter as is of permanent value.

§ 4 DEFECTS OF 'ACADEMIC' CRITICISM

It is the function of literary criticism first to distinguish between those novels which call for serious criticism, and those which are beneath it (Categories I and II). The next task is to distinguish, among novels which call for serious criticism, between those which are good, and those which might have been good but are not (Categories I(a) and I(b))

In the second task we may be helped by such technical apparatus as has been provided for us by Mr. Forster, by Percy Lubbock, by Lord David Cecil or by other academic critics.

In the first task, Mrs. Leavis is right in saying that such terms as Plot and Character, as academically applied, will not be much help in distinguishing those novels which are the fit subject for literary criticism from those which are beneath it. Such terms alone are too often used to assess the slickness of a writer's technique rather than the quality of his mind; and great technical accomplishment can coexist with a very inferior mind.

Mrs. Leavis commands our assent when she writes: 'the essential technique in an art that works by using words is the way in which words are used, and a method is only justified by the use that is made of it; a bad novel is ultimately seen to fail not because of its method but owing to a fatal inferiority in the author's make-up.'[8] She only accounts, however, for those novels which could not possibly, by any means, have been good — for the novels of Category II.

Mr. Denys Thompson puts the case against academic criticism in stronger words: 'Fiction . . . has been accorded little intelligent criticism, most critics being content to appraise the excellence of character-drawing or plot-making, an employment which does not further the business of criticism (to evaluate the quality of the mind to the influence of which we are submitting ourselves); by such tests Edgar Wallace will be as good or better than Shakespeare.'[9]

We shall have to find fault with this statement.

§5 INADEQUACY OF 'PRACTICAL' CRITICISM

In determining the quality of the mind of the novelist, Mr. Wyndham Lewis was one of the first in the field with the 'Cabman's test', demonstrating from the first page of Mr. Huxley's *Point Counterpoint* the kind of sensibility we were to expect in the rest of that novel. Mrs. Leavis (followed by Mr. Thompson) has also done a valuable work in showing how we may apply to passages from works of fiction the kind of analysis applied to poetry by Mr. I. A. Richards in *Practical Criticism*. She recommends as a method for the critic of the novel 'to reinforce a general impression by analysis of significant passages', warning us that sensibility as well as intelligence is required.

But to obtain such a general impression, a more 'academic'

and intellectual method is needed to reinforce the findings of 'Practical Criticism'. And such an impression should not only be an impression of the novelist's mind, but also of how it does its work. It is by no means the only business of criticism 'to evaluate the quality of the mind to the influence of which we are submitting ourselves'; such an evaluation is indeed a vital part of the business, and until it has been done we do not know whether a book is worth further criticism or no — but we have also to ask how such a mind has been used, and if its productions are successful or not. Here it is relevant to 'appraise the excellence of character-drawing or plot-making'. Such terms, even if academically applied, can yet yield some results in determining the difference between Categories I(a) and I(b).

At its worst, a strictly 'academic' method will only distinguish between degrees of competence; at its worst, 'Practical Criticism' will only be a sort of intelligence or sensibility test applied to writers, and will tell us nothing about their specific aptitude for the Novel, nor what they have made of this specific aptitude in particular cases.

It is being maintained that the Novel is a specific literary form, and as the dominant form we saw that it 'tends to attract to itself writers whose talents would have fitted them much better for work of some other kind'. We may say then of Hardy, for example, that he was a great writer but without great specific aptitude for that form which he chose to use for most of his work — not a great novelist. The admirers of his novels admit freely — they cannot avoid it — his failure over plot and character as we generally understand these things when we speak of fiction. They often say that he views the world as a lyric or tragic poet, not as a novelist; they generally imply that a lyric or a tragic poet is a greater thing to be.

Whether a lyric or tragic poet or a novelist be greater, is however a meaningless question. It would depend on the poet and the novelist, and between a great poet and a great novelist one could not determine — between Shelley, for instance, and Miss Austen. This however can, and should be said: Miss Austen's surviving verses (they are few) are not so good as Shelley's, and no one maintains that his novels are equal to hers. When you are writing poetry, it is better to be a poet than a novelist, and when you are writing a novel it is better to be a novelist than a poet.

We are still able to say that Hardy's novels contain great writing, or (if we wish) that they are great books, without having to say that they are great novels. We can say (for example) that *The Return of the Native* is a significant work of art, which *The Heir of Redclyffe* is not; but that *The Heir of Redclyffe* is better, technically, as a novel. Nor must we conclude that the good qualities in *The Heir of Redclyffe* (convincing characterization, and a plot which issues naturally from the characters) are negligible, even from an artistic point of view.

Charlotte Yonge had an immature mind, an undistinguished style, and the values of a pious schoolgirl — there are worse values — but an educated reader cannot now readily surrender his mind to her influence. Nevertheless, she had real literary gifts which anyone might envy, and which, if he possibly could, Hardy ought to have tried to cultivate, since he wished to be a novelist.

Our criticism of the Novel must account not only for cases like Hardy's, but also for the use made of their specific talents by novelists on particular occasions. 'Practical Criticism' alone, with its evaluation of the author's mind, will not provide us with principles on which we can condemn bad work by great writers, empty books on which often a great deal of beautiful work has been wasted — such as *The Outcry*, *The Other House*, and other failures of Henry James's.

Nor can we get on without the terms of Academic criticism when we are assessing novels read in translation — and Mrs. Leavis admits that novels can be translated. If 'the way in which words are used' is the only and final criterion, then English readers who do not know Russian have no right to praise the novels of Tolstoy or Dostoievsky, but only to praise the minds of Louise and Aylmer Maude, or of Constance

Garnett. Yet there is a sufficiently respectable consensus of English opinion that Tolstoy and Dostoievsky are indeed great novelists to have evidential value.[10]

We need not take up in detail Mr. Thompson's assertion that plot and character analysis would make out Edgar Wallace better than Shakespeare, until he provides us with such an analysis, exhibiting such a conclusion. Meanwhile, if his general meaning is that the contemporary detective-story would come out high on such an analysis, we need not be shocked. It deserves some credit, as one of the better-made things of our time. 'We see covering the earth,' writes M. Jean Paulhan, not without satisfaction, 'the one contemporary genre which obeys rules stricter than the tragedy of Voltaire, or the ode of Malherbe. I am thinking of that kind of novel which forbids itself, in the psychological order, dreams, reveries, presentiments; in the choice of personages, the meta-physician, the occultist, the member of a Secret Society, the Hindu, the Chinaman, the Malay Twins; in the explication, myths, allusions, symbols; in the figures of style, metaphor and ellipse — and follows, in its progress, an order rigorous to the point of offering, from the first chapter, *all* the elements — personages, places, objects — of a problem which will not be resolved before the last pages.'[11]

One can imagine not only Aristotle, but also Henry James, echoing this satisfaction.

§6 THE NECESSITY OF A COMBINATION
OF THESE METHODS

If an analysis of their character-drawing or plot-making were to set Edgar Wallace above Shakespeare, then it could only be because such terms had been very crudely applied. Such absurd conclusions would no more invalidate the terms of 'Academic' criticism than a student's bungling attempts at 'Practical' criticism would invalidate the methods suggested by Mr. I. A. Richards.

In fact a sensitive and intelligent examination of a novel requires a combination of 'Academic' and 'Practical' criticism.

Analysis of selected passages, on Mr. Richards's lines, in terms of 'Sense, Feeling, Tone and Intention', is an invaluable test of the quality of the novelist's mind. Analysis of a novel in terms of plot and character, is an invaluable test of the writer's specific aptitude as a novelist, and of his achievement on this particular occasion — moreover it is by this form of analysis that passages are best selected for detailed analysis on Mr. Richards's lines. Analysis of such passages would then give greater depth and authority to the analysis of plot and character, and might tell us as much in the end about the structure and content of the book as about its texture. An adaptation of such a critical technique would enable us to make critical pronouncements on authors like Tolstoy or Dostoievsky, whose texture, if we do not know Russian, must remain hidden from us.

Mrs. Leavis, although she attacks the use of the term 'character', yet provides us with some help in restoring the currency of this term — if she were writing criticism she would find that she could not do without it.

Her objections may as well be set out here, and answered.

(1) Character is the creation of the reader, not of the writer. 'Apparently all a novelist need do is to provide bold outlines, and the reader will co-operate to persuade himself that he is in contact with "real people".'[12]

A little analysis here, directed to passages in which a character is established, would reveal in each case whether the author had given it vitality and idiosyncracy, or whether he had left that work to the reader.

(2) The demand on the part of the reader for plausible or likeable characters prevents enjoyment of such novelists as Jane Austen or Emily Brontë.

The vulgar demand for 'likeable' characters in no way invalidates the use of the term 'character', which by no means implies conventional pleasantness. Jane Austen in creating Emma, and consciously occupied with character-creation, was aware that she was making a character whom most of her readers might dislike.

While to the objection that characters need not be conventionally plausible, Mrs. Leavis has herself made the best possible answer: 'This is not to say that we do not — and rightly — require the author to preserve internal consistency (as in *Wuthering Heights*), so that Masson was perfectly justified in complaining in his *British Novelists and their Styles* (1859): "The very element in which the novelist works is human nature; yet what sort of Psychology have we in the ordinary run of novels? A Psychology, if the truth must be spoken, such as would not hold good in a world of imaginary cats".'[13]

We need no further admission to re-establish the term 'character'.

(3) Mrs. Leavis believes that an interest in 'character' contributes to the 'resentful bewilderment one notices in the objections to such novelists as Virginia Woolf and Henry James, who do not offer anything in the nature of "character".'[14]

Of the first-mentioned of these two novelists we must say boldly that, while a great artist, she was not a great novelist — and that precisely because she lacked the novelist's specific gifts. Moreover, her greatest achievement is *To the Lighthouse*, a book marked out from all her others by the magnificent characterization of Mr. and Mrs. Ramsay.

Of Henry James, we must deny that the creator of such figures as Mrs. Gereth, Fleda Vetch, Maisie, Mrs. Wix, Mrs. Beale, Sir Claude, Mrs. Brook or Strether — to name only a few — offers nothing in the way of character. How bitterly he would have resented such a charge!

A reason for the modern revulsion from that kind of criticism which is based on the study of plot and character, may be found in the present state of Shakespeare studies. There is a strong reaction from that kind of criticism of which Bradley's

Shakespearian Tragedy is the climax. A parallel reaction may be discovered in the criticism of the novel.

There are two reasons for resisting such a reaction in the criticism of the novel. In the first place the reaction against Bradley is largely due to the fact that he is so good: further work along his lines is apt to be unprofitable when Shakespeare is the subject[15] — this does not mean that this type of analysis is exhausted where fiction is concerned. In the second place, Shakespeare was not a nineteenth-century author — he is far away from us, we do not quite know what he was trying to do. Such theorists as Miss Spurgeon or Professor Wilson Knight will each have something to tell us about him: there must be much that escapes a nineteenth-century plot-character analysis. On the other hand, Jane Austen and Flaubert were nineteenth-century authors. A form of criticism derived from nineteenth-century novelists, though of doubtful applicability to Shakespeare, is of certain applicability to nineteenth-century novelists.

The fact remains that novelists have generally conceived it to be their business to draw characters, and to make them behave within the limits of some sort of plot. It is therefore temerarious in the extreme to reject these terms, and to put out of court all the evidence that can be collected about the way in which novelists have set about their business.

It is never the artist's purpose (if he is a good artist) to exhibit his exquisite sensibility, but always to *make* something. His sensibility cannot avoid showing itself in the thing made, and perhaps will be the source of that beauty which, as Mr. Forster has reminded us, is always to be found in a great novel, but can never be the object of the novelist's direct pursuit. The relation between the two is somewhat analogous to that between the tune and the words of 'Uncle's' song in *War and Peace.*

' "Uncle" sang as peasants sing, with full and naive conviction that the whole meaning of a song lies in the words, and that the tune comes of itself, and that apart from the words there is no tune, which exists only to give measure to the words. As a result of this, the unconsidered tune, like the song of a bird, was extraordinarily good.'[16]

Probably novelists most often work with the full and naive conviction that the whole meaning of a novel lies in the plot and characters; and probably those who no longer hold this full and naive conviction would do well to act as if they did.

§7 WHAT WRITERS HAVE TO TELL US ABOUT THEIR WORK

A further contribution to the criticism of fiction may be made by a study of the creative act in fiction, and of what novelists tell us about it. We may expect to know more about novels if we learn more about how they have been made.

It may seem like a presumptuous undertaking: there is some degree of mystery involved in creation. Are we making what Edith Wharton called: 'the fascinating but probably idle attempt to discover *how it is all done*, and exactly what happens at that "fine point of the soul" where the creative act, like the mystic's union with the unknowable, really seems to take place'?[17] Certainly novelists do not always know how they have done it;[18] their subsequent accounts of how they have written their books are not always perfectly convincing.

Nevertheless, even if everything cannot be known, something can be known. Even 'the mystic's union with the unknowable' is a subject about which there is a considerable body of literature, much of which is illuminating. And writers have in one way or another told us a good deal about their work; and about their aims, methods and inspiration. Even if the accounts they give are not always implicitly to be accepted, yet they remain the first and best authority.

It appears to be a popular fallacy that writers are not at all aware of what they are doing, and that the psycho-analyst knows better than they. An objection to psycho-analytical criticism is that it can only operate upon an author's written work: to be thorough, it would have to call him up for an oral examination. Dead authors are safe from this, and it is unlikely that any living author would submit to such impertinence. Moreover we shall see in the next chapter that an author's range may not be anything like so extensive as his experience. The psycho-analyst, confronted only with written work, will have a severely limited material to deal with.[19]

About the making of poetry we really know a great deal, and our knowledge might be further increased by a systematic study of what we already know. The creative act in fiction has been less studied, but, proportionately, there are even more documents for such a study. For more than two thousand six hundred years Poetry has been written that still matters to us; the prose fiction that matters to us has all been written in the last two hundred years. And it is in the last two hundred years that artists have been most self-conscious.

We need not hesitate to endorse these rather cautious words of Virginia Woolf: 'Nothing indeed was ever said by the artist himself about his state of mind till the eighteenth century perhaps. Rousseau perhaps began it. At any rate, by the nineteenth century self-consciousness had developed so far that it was the habit of men of letters to describe their minds in confessions and autobiographies. Their lives also were written, and their letters were printed after their deaths. Thus, though we do not know what Shakespeare went through when he wrote *Lear*, we do know what Carlyle went through when he wrote the *French Revolution*; what Flaubert went through when he wrote *Madame Bovary*; what Keats was going through when he tried to write poetry against the coming of death and the indifference of the world.'[20]

The present study aims at making some use of the information which many writers, great and small, have left us about their art, about the raw material presented to them by life, about the form they wished to impose on it, about their struggles with it, and about those gifts of inspiration which have seemed to come to them from nowhere.

NOTES

There is an intention of being useful. The critic and the general reader may hope to learn something about the novel from seeing how some novels have been made. A writer may hope to become less bad from a study of the procedure of good writers. And any attempt to treat the novelist seriously, as an artist, not as a medium or a reporter,[21] is at the present time a service, however humble, to literature.

NOTES

1. *Our Present Philosophy of Life*, p. 43.
2. *Aspects of the Novel*, p. 41.
3. *After Many a Summer.*
4. loc. cit., pp. 115-16.
5. *The Allegory of Love*, pp. 232-3.
6. The terms 'highbrow', 'middlebrow' and 'lowbrow' are not euphonious, but there are no exact synonyms for them. Their use in criticism is further sanctioned by Virginia Woolf, who has given a convenient definition of them, v. *The Death of the Moth*, pp. 113 ff.
7. *Fiction and the Reading Public*, p. 70 f.
8. ibid., p. 232 f.
9. *Reading and Discrimination*, p. 34. This is a useful, little book for school use; but the limitations of its form (as here) make it unfortunately dogmatic.
10. It is true that caution is always required in the judgment of translated literature. Those who support the inflated reputation of Thomas Mann would do well to reflect on the following 'great' English novels that have won serious consideration in France: *La Renarde*, by Mary Webb; *Contrepoint*, by Aldous Huxley; *Un Cyclone à la Jamaique*, by Richard Hughes; *Le Sombre Miroir*, by March Cost; *Intempéries*, by Rosamund Lehmann.
11. *Les Fleurs de Tarbes* (1941), pp. 167-8.
12. loc. cit., p. 59.
13. loc. cit., p. 324.
14. loc. cit., pp. 60-1.
15. e.g. such a book as the late Professor Gordon's *Shakespearian Comedy*, with its futile speculations about the mothers of Shakespeare's heroines.

16. Book VII, chapter vii.
17. *A Backward Glance* (1934), p. 121.
18. Evidence from two very different sources may here suffice. 'Blessed is the novelist who has no idea how he has done it', *Letters of J. M. Barrie*, December 25th, 1893.
    'M.J. . . . "I like to know how people work."
    I.C.B. "I daresay you do, but the people themselves are not always quite sure." '
    A conversation between I. Compton-Burnett and M. Jourdain, Orion (1945), p. 26.
19. Literary research can sometimes refute the findings of psychoanalysis, as Professor Livingston Lowes in *The Road to Xanadu* has refuted Mr. Robert Graves's analysis of *Kubla Khan*. Appendix II of this book seeks to do the same thing for the 'Freudian' theory of *The Turn of the Screw*.
20. *A Room of One's Own*, pp. 77-8.
21. 'Ainsi vont les Lettres, balancées du journaliste au médium', Jean Paulhan, *Les Fleurs de Tarbes*, p. 39.

CHAPTER II

THE NOVELIST'S RANGE

§ I SELECTION: WHAT THE NOVELIST LEAVES OUT

THE word 'range' is here generally to be understood as it is
understood in another modern art, photography. No two arts
run parallel very far, and we shall drop the language of
photography when it ceases to help us; but some thoughts will
be suggested by it before we have to discard it.

Some novelists have borrowed this language. Mr. Christopher Isherwood writes: 'I am a camera with its shutter open,
quite passive, recording not thinking. Recording the man
shaving at the window opposite and the woman in the kimono
washing her hair. Some day, all this will have to be developed,
carefully fixed, printed.'[1]

Flaubert on one occasion seems to have become a camera
fitted with a green or a yellow filter, for he writes: 'Do you
know how I passed a whole afternoon the day before yesterday?
In looking at the countryside through coloured glasses. I
needed it for a page of my *Bovary*, which will not, I think, be one
of the worse pages.'[2]

If some novelists have repudiated the suggestion that they
were photographers, they have generally meant that they were
not mere photographers, not merely turning a gaping lens
uncritically upon life, and producing an uninspired copy of
unselected material. This is what Hardy means. He writes:
'As in looking at a carpet, by following one colour a certain
pattern is suggested, by following another colour, another:
so in life the seer should watch the pattern among general
things which his idiosyncracy moves him to observe, and
describe that alone. This is quite accurately a going to Nature,

yet the result is no mere photograph, but purely the product of the writer's own mind.'[3]

Photography considered as an art is, however, no longer *mere* photography, but also, like fiction, a search for significant form. Good photographers watch that pattern among general things which their idiosyncrasy moves them to observe, and their work is as far from a cheap postcard street-scene as a great novelist's writing is from journalism, or from the dreary rapportage which has in England lately done duty for the short story.

The photographer has the same task of selection as Hardy himself had, and these words of Hardy's are true of both arts: 'The recent school of novel-writers forget in their insistence on life, and nothing but life, in a plain slice, that a story must be worth the telling, that a good deal of life is not worth any such thing, and that they must not occupy the reader's time with what he can get at first hand anywhere about him.'[4] The picture must be worth making, the story worth telling, and what makes them worth while is precisely the pattern or inscape.

When Hardy wrote his notes, some years ago, he probably intended such writers as Arnold Bennett when he spoke of 'the recent school'. With even more justice his words can be applied to a more recent school, to those writers who in the fourth decade of this century filled such periodicals as *New Writing* with purely documentary accounts of the lives of industrial workers, into which imagination seldom or never entered. It was claimed that they were extending the range of art to include sides of life in which other writers had not been interested, and that such writers had 'escaped' into art from life. Unfortunately, though new facts were piled up, the range of art was in no way extended; these story-writers failed to give them significant form. It was they who were escapers, but they had escaped from art into life — a much more suicidal flight for an artist.

If you go out with your camera, and open the shutter at random, you will not make beautiful or interesting photographs. You must carefully compose your picture. And quite as important a problem as the difficulty of getting in those objects which you wish to get in, is the difficulty of leaving out what you wish to leave out. So it is in the composition of a novel. 'Life', says Henry James, 'has no direct sense whatever for the subject, and is capable ... of nothing but splendid waste.'[5]

Life gives the material, yes; but not when or how the artist wants it. Those who lie in wait for wild animals with their cameras have to wait long and patiently for results, and often fail to get the results they are waiting for.

Flaubert went to the funeral of the wife of a friend of his, like Charles Bovary a doctor; and, like Madame Bovary, the woman had died suddenly. 'Perhaps I shall get something for my *Bovary*,' he wrote to a friend before he went. 'This exploitation to which I shall give myself up would seem hateful if one owned to it; but what is there wrong in it? I hope to make the tears of others flow with the tears of one man, passed through the chemistry of style.'[6]

When he got there, all he met with was a bore, who asked him foolish questions about the public libraries of Egypt, a country which he had lately visited. The bereavement of his friend, which he had come to witness, was quite put in the background by the boringness of this bore. 'Decidedly, God is a romantic,' complained Flaubert of this mixture of the tragic and comic. 'He is continually mixing the genres.'[7]

The attitude of the real novelist, not the reporter or the propagandist, to his material, may be summed up in the words which Mark Twain humorously attributes to Herodotus: 'Many things do not happen as they ought, and most things do not happen at all. It is for the conscientious historian to correct these defects.'

The large, the obvious subject is not necessarily that which most appeals to the trained eye. Catherine Morland in *Northanger Abbey* was astonished and upset to learn this, when she was first introduced to the laws of composition and of the picturesque. 'The little she could understand ... appeared to contradict the very few notions she had entertained on the matter before. It seemed as if a good view were no longer to be taken from the top of a high hill, and that a clear blue sky was no longer a proof of a fine day.' But presently she learned so fast that 'she voluntarily rejected the whole city of Bath as unworthy to make part of a landscape'.

Similarly Jane Austen voluntarily rejected the Napoleonic wars as unworthy to enter into her picture of contemporary life. She has often, and very foolishly, been condemned for this. On the other hand in our dreary fiction of the 'thirties the mere shadow of a coming war is all-important: many writers were constantly saying that they felt it a duty to express the contemporary situation. Had they left this aspect of the situation to statesmen, and had statesmen been equally enthusiastic about dealing with it, we might be happier to-day, and we might have pleasanter books to read.

To return to Jane Austen, it is not easy to see how the Napoleonic Wars could be fitted into the plot of *Emma*; there are however readers who have felt that they could be taken out of *War and Peace* or *La Chartreuse de Parme* with some advantage.

§ 2 WHAT THE NOVELIST LEAVES IN: CHOICE OF SUBJECT

After speaking of what the novelist leaves out, we must now look at what he leaves in — what he chooses as his subject. Inevitably this means another return to Flaubert, the 'true Penelope', as Ezra Pound calls him.

> His true Penelope was Flaubert,
> He fished by obstinate isles;
> Observed the elegance of Circe's hair
> Rather than the mottoes on sundials.

He says of himself, comparing himself with Ulysses the wanderer. The 'obstinate isles' may represent the snares of public life, and 'Circe's hair' those of private life: at all events he did not heed 'the mottoes on sundials', which generally remind us, in one language or another, that time is short. But as Ulysses always tended towards Penelope, his faithful wife, who at home in rocky Ithaca rejected the blandishments of her suitors, and occupied herself with weaving a shroud for her father-in-law Laertes, which she unpicked every night — so the wandering artist still felt his true ideal was Flaubert, the patient hermit of literature, alone in Normandy, scratching out his manuscript, and beginning again and again.

These lines express what many must have felt about Flaubert — the patron saint and doctor of the Novel.

'A good subject for a novel,' says Flaubert, 'is one that comes all in one piece, in one single jet. It is the mother-idea, whence all the rest flow. One is not at all free to write this or that. One does not choose one's subject. That is what the public and the critics do not understand. The secret of masterpieces lies in the concordance between the subject and the temperament of the author.'[8]

To say of a novel that it is good, or even beautiful, in parts, is ultimately a condemnation. In so many novels in which there are beautiful passages, this essential concordance between the subject and the author's temperament is lacking; worse, there is no single subject. Perhaps Henry James was the last English novelist to receive a subject all in one piece, in a single jet.

When this miracle has taken place, then we have a novel conceived with the sort of radiance that happiness can shed round a human being. Such a novel is like Emma Bovary herself, at the height of her passion for Rodolphe: 'She had that indefinable beauty which comes from joy, from enthusiasm, from success, and which is simply the harmony of the temperament with outward circumstances.' This is the harmony we feel in perfect novels, in *Emma*, in *Madame Bovary*, in *The Spoils of Poynton*.

Any novel conceived without this harmony inevitably must fall short of classical perfection. It may be a romantic, lop-sided structure, with certain beauties of its own which would not be possible in a classically perfect novel. But there are limits beyond which tastes may not be allowed to differ, and yet still be called taste. It is not permissible to prefer Westminster Abbey to the Parthenon, if you have seen the Parthenon; though you may rightly love them both. Similarly one may and should admire such romantic structures as the novels of Hardy and George Eliot, which contain certain excellences inseparable from gravely imperfect plots, and in some cases from preposterous distortion of character. Of such novels it should be said that their beauties more than justify their existence, and that they (at any rate the best of them) are perhaps as good as they could be, allowing for the original fault in their conception. They are infinitely better than lifeless copies of classically perfect novels would be. To some eyes their very distortion has an appeal, like that of pots swollen to odd and fascinating shapes by faulty baking. But when all has been said and done for them, they cannot be placed with those lovely and harmonious works that are the highest achievement of the novelist's art.

§3 THE NOVELIST'S 'RANGE' DISTIN-
GUISHED FROM HIS 'EXPERIENCE'

Lord David Cecil in his recent book on Hardy excellently defines and limits the novelist's range in his choice of a subject. 'A novel', he writes, 'is a work of art in so far as it introduces us into a living world; in some respects resembling the world we live in, but with an individuality of its own. Now this world owes its character to the fact that it is begotten by the artist's creative faculty on his experience. His imagination apprehends reality in such a way as to present us with a new vision of it. But in any one artist only some aspects of his experience fertilize his imagination, strike sufficiently deep down into the fundamentals of his personality to kindle his creative spark. His achievement, therefore, is limited to that part of his work which deals with these aspects of his experience.'[9]

The metaphors are mixed. Lord David Cecil appears uncertain which is the masculine, and which the feminine principle. But for all that, the distinction between the novelist's range and his experience is valuable.

The word *Experience*, like the word *Life*, is much abused in contemporary writing about artists. It appears to mean to most critics Doing or Suffering, but oddly enough only Doing or Suffering in the External world, not in the Mind, where the worst is done or suffered.

> ... The mind, mind has mountains, cliffs of fall
> Frightful, sheer, no-man-fathomed, hold them cheap
> May who ne'er hung there ...

And so they are held cheap by those who perhaps never hung there, and who call Experience that which is done or suffered in the world where men and women fight, and drink and make love. This Experience they speak of as a sort of stuff to which the artist is more or less passively exposed — and they hold that the more he is exposed to the better.

There are two capital errors here. In the first place, what is important to an artist is not his experience but his range. 'Only some aspects of his experience fertilize his imagination, strike sufficiently deep down into the fundamentals of his personality to kindle the creative spark': these aspects alone are within his range. Early life has probably so conditioned him that he cannot greatly extend his range; the intelligent course is to find out what his range is, and to keep within it. But everyone can, if he pleases, extend his experience. If, for instance, an artist has never gone up in a balloon, then he can go up in one. But if (as is most probable) ballooning turns out not to be one of those aspects of his experience that fertilize his imagination, it will profit him nothing.

In the second place, the artist never passively receives experience. If the novelist can be like a camera at times, then he can only be like one of those primitive, nineteenth-century, hand-made cameras, of which no two were alike. Mr. Isherwood may have thought he was 'a camera with its shutter open, quite passive, recording, not thinking', but, whether consciously or no, he was also selecting. Experience is not merely that which life places in front of us, it is that which the experiencing eye chooses to let through into the brain; and even before it is consciously worked on, it undergoes considerable transmutation.

§4 THE PARABLE OF THE NOVELISTS AND THE CRIPPLE

One would like to place several authors in front of the same experience; that is, to provide them with the same external data, and to test both their reactions at the time, and their subsequent final versions of them. We cannot do this; but we are in a position to look at the similar experiences of three different novelists in a half-digested state — much as a radiologist examines, half-way, our digestion of a cup of barium. We must see what we can learn from what we may call 'the parable of the novelist and the cripple'.

We have records of three novelists passing in front of a cripple. They have left not their immediate impressions, which of course they could not have recorded without some distortion, but they have left half-digested versions in intimate letters to friends. We are looking at their experience somewhere near half-way between the actual impression when it was given, and its fixed and developed and printed state, in which they might have offered it to the public.

Here is the first novelist: 'I was out this evening to call on a friend and, coming back through the wet, crowded, lamp-lit streets, was singing after my own fashion *Du hast Diamanten und Perlen*, when I heard a poor cripple man in the gutter wailing over a pitiful Scotch air, his club-foot supported on the other knee, and his whole woe-begone body propped sideways against a crutch. The nearest lamp threw a strong light on his worn, sordid face and the three boxes of lucifer matches he held for sale. My own false notes stuck in my chest. How well off I am! — is the burden of my songs all day long — *Drum ist so wohl mir in der Welt!* And the ugly reality of the cripple man was an intrusion on the beautiful world in which I was walking. He could no more sing than I could; and his voice was cracked and rusty, and altogether perished. To think that wreck may have walked the streets some night, years ago, as glad at heart as I was, and promising himself a future as golden and honourable!'[10]

Here is the second novelist: 'Strange the sea was, so strong, I saw a soldier on the pier, with only one leg. He was strong and handsome: and strangely self-conscious, and slightly ostentatious but confused. As yet he does not realize anything, he is still in the shock. And he is strangely roused by the women, who seem to have a craving for him. They look at him with eyes of longing, and they want to talk to him. So he is roused, like a roused male, yet there is more wistfulness and wonder than passion or desire. I could see him under chloroform having the leg amputated. It was still in his face. But he was brown, and strong, and handsome.'[11]

Here is the third novelist (if we may use the term for a writer of short stories): 'On Bank Holiday, mingling with the crowd I saw a magnificent sailor outside a public house. He was a cripple; his legs were crushed, but his head was beautiful — youthful and proud. On his bare chest two seagulls fighting were tattooed in red and blue. And he seemed to lift himself — above the tumbling wave of people, and he sang: *Heart of mine, summer is waning.* Oh! Heavens, I shall never forget how he looked and how he sang. I knew it at the time, "this is one of the things one will always remember". It clutched my heart. It flies on the wind to-day — one of those voices, you know, crying above the talk and the laughter and the dust and the toys to sell: "Life is wonderful — wonderful — bitter-sweet, an anguish and a joy" — and "Oh! I do not want to be resigned — I want to drink deeply — deeply. Shall I ever be able to express it." '[12]

The three pictures are different enough, though the three

writers are all romantic in their treatment of the subject. Yet had they not been speaking of three cripples, but of one and the same, the differences might have been as great. He might have appeared to the first writer (Stevenson, in Edinburgh) as remembering former joys, and to the second (Lawrence, at Bognor) as a magnificent, maimed, male animal — as symbolic as the stallion in one of his stories, whom his owner (very sensibly) wanted to geld, because he was too wild. He might have appeared to the third writer (Katherine Mansfield, in London) as symbolic of the diversity of life — of the bewildering fact round which she wrote her story, *The Garden-Party*, that Love and Death and Pain and Happiness all go on at the same time, and in the same place.

Beside these three cripples, recorded in writers' correspondence, it may be of interest to set a finished portrait — that of the 'poor devil' who limped about the inn yard at Rouen, where Emma Bovary took the diligence home to Yonville every Thursday, after her visit to her lover.

'A mass of rags covered his shoulders, and an old staved-in beaver, rounded like a basin, hid his face; but when he took it off he discovered in the place of eyelids empty and bloody orbits. The flesh hung in red shreds, and there flowed from it liquids that congealed into green scales down to the nose, whose black nostrils sniffed convulsively. To speak to you he threw back his head with an idiotic laugh; then his bluish eyeballs, rolling constantly, beat at the temples against the edge of the open wound. He sang a little song as he followed the carriages:

> Maids in the warmth of a summer day
> Dream of love, and of love alway.

And all the rest was about birds and sunshine and green leaves.'[13]

The range of the novelist, that is those parts of his experience which he is able to use creatively, is probably a matter over which he possesses little control. It has generally been dictated to him by his nature or his early environment. The importance of early environment in determining a writer's range could be proved over and over again. Two direct statements may here suffice.

'At present my mind works with the most freedom and the keenest sense of poetry in my remotest past,' wrote George Eliot. 'And there are many strata to be worked through before I can begin to use artistically any material I may gather in the present.'[14] It may be doubted if she ever managed to use artistically any material gathered after her early middle life.

Katherine Mansfield, after the shock of her brother's death, returned to her early New Zealand memories, the source of most of her best stories. 'The people who lived, or whom I wished to bring into my stories don't interest me any more. The plots of my stories leave me perfectly cold. Granted that the people exist and all the differences, complexities and resolutions are true to them — why should I write about them. They are not near me . . . Now — now I want to write recollections of my own country. Yes, I want to write about my own country till I simply exhaust my store.'[15]

The novelist generally wants to write about his own country, mental, social or geographical, and no other is equally interesting to him.

Of those forces which can extend the writer's range, the most powerful is grief — Flaubert and Proust are agreed that the chief value to him of love is that it makes suffering possible. However if a writer were to make a voluntary pursuit of suffering in order to improve his work, it would hardly answer that end; it is sufficient to take the less heroic course of waiting for it.[16]

§6 A NOVELIST MAY USE HIS RANGE TO ITS LIMITS: FORSTER, ISHERWOOD, MAUGHAM

Though a novelist generally cannot extend his range, there are two things he can do. He can accept his limitations, and not court certain disaster by going outside his range; and sometimes by ingenious choosing of a position he can get far more within his range than might be expected. The first, the negative acceptance of limitations, is far the more important; it has been the principle behind the production of great works of art. The second, the ingenious choosing of a position in order to get the greatest amount possible within the novelist's range, is sometimes felicitous, sometimes results merely in clever virtuosity, and always makes the novelist's final limitations, beyond which he cannot go, all the more obvious.

We shall look first at some novelists who try to squeeze as much as possible into their limited picture. All novelists have not the wide-angled lens, the panoramic range of Tolstoy. Mr. Forster, for instance, stands patiently waiting while Man, ever restless and irregular, about this earth doth run and ride; in the end the creature will be tired, and will want his tea; then is Mr. Forster's hour. The creature will come within his view-finder, and his shutter will click.

Mr. Isherwood, writing of Mr. Forster, speaks of his talent for 'tea-tabling' incidents.[17] What he means is this; in any series of events, however dreadful, the worst tragedies can always be regarded as taking place between meals. People may go mad, elope, be accidentally killed — but it is certain that those who are left will sooner or later want something to eat.[18] Mr. Forster has chosen, and wisely, for it is his range, to represent events very much as they appear to people at their meals — his characters see them and speak of them in the kind of frame of mind in which they drink their tea. This is a legitimate and useful viewpoint, but it is strictly limited.

For example, a novelist may require violence to take place —
it shakes up the plot and the characters, and they settle down
after it in new and interesting positions. Mr. Forster writes in
Aspects of the Novel,[19] that in the domain of violent physical
action, Jane Austen is feeble and ladylike. She was a novelist
of character, and now and then needed to shake up her people.
He is a novelist of situation, and uses violence from time to
time to achieve it. But a rattle of spoons, and a storm in a
teacup is what ensues. Violence is out of place at a tea-table;
and in the domain of violent physical action Mr. Forster is no
more at home than Miss Austen. Whether he goes too far into
the domain of violence and passion, which is not his, and looks
lost and unhappy, or whether he goes as far as he safely can, and
halts rather wistfully at the boundary, Mr. Forster equally
strongly stresses his limitations.

Two other contemporary novelists illustrate the virtuosity of
an artist who, by shifting his position, or by choosing a particularly artful stand-point, can bring a puzzling variety of
objects within a limited range. One is not used to seeing them
compared, and yet the comparison might be expected to be a
commonplace of criticism. They have both given careful study
to technique, and have even published histories of their several
formations as novelists. They have both learned something
from writing for the stage. Their style, in each case the fruit
of years of study, is singularly clear and apparently artless —
they excel at speaking impersonally in the first person singular.
They have had, they have deliberately courted, a varied
experience. At first sight they seem to have a lot to write
about. But if we look carefully at their work, we find a fore-
shortening of many aspects of life, in order to get them in. We
may find, perhaps, the background falling away, because they
have been obliged to tilt their narrow-angled lenses upwards
in an attempt to get everything into the picture. We may find
bodies with their heads cut off, and heads lacking bodies and
legs. They both have very limited ranges, are both extremely
ingenious in their manipulation, both constantly overreach

themselves. Their failures make us suspect their successes of being no more than technical triumphs.

It must have been obvious that these two novelists are Mr. Somerset Maugham and Mr. Christopher Isherwood.

§7 A NOVELIST MAY WORK WELL WITHIN HIS RANGE: JANE AUSTEN

A novelist writing absolutely in the middle of his true range will be writing his best, like a singer singing in the best part of his register. It is a temptation to stretch and strain; critics will praise a writer for a wide range, for it is an easy and obvious thing for them to distinguish.[20] Moreover, every artist must take some pleasure in mere technical accomplishment, and ought to have exercised himself in it; when he is practised in the gymnastic of his art, it is very natural for him to yield to the temptation to give his public a gymnastic display.

Of the artist who really knows his range, and sticks to it, the supreme example is Jane Austen. Everyone knows the story of the Prince Regent's librarian, who tried to tempt her into writing 'an historical romance illustrative of the august house of Coburg'. Everyone knows her admirable reply that such a book might well be more popular than such pictures of domestic life in country villages as she dealt in, but that she could no more write a romance than an epic poem. 'No,' she wrote, 'I must keep to my own style, and go on in my own way; and though I may never succeed again in that, I am convinced that I should totally fail in any other.' She went on, and she wrote *Persuasion*.

Of the wisdom of knowing how to work within a limited range, Jane Austen's works are the triumphant proof — she gives us no blurred, formless panorama, but a neat, perfectly composed, sharply focused picture. And she shows that it is not width of vision but depth that is important. In the small section of humanity that she has chosen to depict, she has given us the greatest of English comic characters. And in the marriages of her ladylike young women with her eligible young men, she has combined a great variety of incident with a corresponding variety and delicacy of feeling. No attentive reader of *Mansfield Park* or *Persuasion* can deny her power to depict physical passion.

That she had temptations towards a larger world one can hardly doubt. Her hard, eighteenth-century humour, the exuberance of her early writings such as *Love and Freindship*, and an occasional passage in the serious novels where a touch of Fielding's racy, knock-me-down violence proves her his heiress, all suggest that she may at times have wanted the big world of *Tom Jones*. The daughter of an eighteenth-century parsonage did not know many aspects of that world, and knew that she did not know them. A modern lady-novelist (one fears) might in her position have complained that women did not have their rights. Miss Austen was not a person to complain. Within her small world — and it was not so small as it is often made out — she had known affection, boredom, anxiety, love and loss, hatred and impatience. That is quite enough experience on which to set up as a novelist, if one has the mind.

§ 8 A NOVELIST WILL ERR IN GOING OUTSIDE
HIS RANGE : HARDY AND OTHERS

In contrast with Miss Austen's spirit of self-sacrifice, and of resignation to her lot, we must look at novelists who have strained to extend their range.

There is the melancholy case of Hardy, who deliberately tried to move in higher society for the sake of learning its speech and manners. We know how unsuccessful he was at painting it; he might just as well have stayed at home, instead of going to those dinner-parties at which he was so shy and unhappy. And there are the brothers Goncourt, who spent so much time and energy researching into the lives of people in different walks of life, in order to write realistic novels about them. Yet so slight was their grasp on reality that they never even noticed that their own servant was robbing them right and left, was continually drunk, and had had two children by the milkman. When these facts were drawn to their attention, after her death, they investigated them with the utmost conscientiousness, and wrote a novel about her.

In our own time we have seen authors making as melancholy researches as those of Hardy, but (like the Goncourts) at the lower end of the social scale. Their parents (like those of Mr. Stephen Spender) have 'kept them from children who were rough', in their early impressionable years. Now that 'proletarian' writing is fashionable, they vainly try to mix with and to understand the viewpoint of industrial workers — but it will never be real enough to them for them to be able to write well about it.

It cannot be doubted that many writers have chosen to concern themselves with 'proletarian' themes, not merely to be in the fashion, but also out of a genuine concern for the lot of people less fortunate than themselves. We may, to a certain extent admire them for this altruism. But there are some things which writers are not entitled to sacrifice for the good of people less fortunate than themselves, or indeed for any cause whatever. They may not sacrifice their artistic integrity. If they do so under the impression that they are obeying the dictates of their social consciences, then their social consciences are diseased — for the duty of a writer to the community, as a writer, is simply this: to write as well as he can. If he goes outside his range, he will fail to fulfil this duty.

§9 THE NOVELIST SHOULD RESIST ALL TEMPTATIONS OR EXHORTATIONS TO GO BEYOND HIS RANGE

Lord David Cecil has well summed up this part of the novelist's duty. 'The artist's first obligation is to his vision rather than to his moral point of view ... The artist must stick to his range, whatever is fidgeting his conscience. And even when writing within his range, he must be careful not to point his moral so ostentatiously that it diverts our attention from the imaginary world he has created. Indeed his moral views are best left to reveal themselves involuntarily. The artist's only conscious duty should be to the truth of his creative vision. Every other consideration must be sacrificed to it.'[21]

This is not to posit any sort of unnatural isolation for the novelist. He may live much the same sort of life as other people; he must have some links with the world, which provides his material, and while he is in actual contact with it, he probably looks at it in very much the same way as other people do. His life is swayed by political and economic forces, and by the weather; he is subject to hatred and love, hope, fear and desire.

But when he comes to write, then there is real isolation, as real as that of a man who has shut out the world in order to pray. 'Do not live in an ivory tower,' Salvador de Madariaga has advised, 'but always write in one.' Flaubert, the priest of the ivory tower, had no other meaning, 'Let us shut our door,' he says, 'let us climb to the top of our ivory tower, to the last step, the nearest to heaven. It is cold there, sometimes, isn't it? But who cares! One sees the stars shine clear, and one no longer hears the turkey-cocks.'[22] A writer may gather experience in the world, but it is in the 'ivory tower' that he learns what part of his experience falls within his range.

Never, since it first became a respectable art-form, has so much nonsense been talked about the Novel as in our own day. We are told, even by people who should know better, that it is a function of the novelist to interpret the present age to us, or to prepare us for the world of the future — whereas, as likely as not, the slow, digestive process of art is now only just enabling him to use his experience of many years past. A creative writer cannot keep pace with the world;[23] he is, as we have seen, an old-fashioned camera, needing to be carefully focused, and capable of giving an exquisite and original picture of a subject within his range — he is not a cine-camera, and it is not he who will present current events to the eyes and ears of the world. There are others to do that office, and if they do it well or ill is no concern of his.

For the novelist, as it was affirmed at the beginning of this book, is a creative artist. It is his business not to teach or to reform, but to convey to the world in the best chosen language the most thorough knowledge of human nature, the happiest delineation of its varieties, and the liveliest effusions of wit and humour.

It may be objected that the novelist's range has been severely limited. Yes, each individual novelist has a limited range, if he have not the wide, panoramic lens of Tolstoy — and it is not to be desired that he should have, for Tolstoy lost as much in form and precision as he gained in content and movement.

But in limiting the range of each novelist, we are not limiting the range of the novel in general. Though each writer can only illuminate certain facets of the truth, yet there is no facet of the truth which there may not one day be found a novelist to illuminate. 'The proper stuff of fiction,' said Virginia Woolf, 'does not exist, everything is the proper stuff of fiction.'[24] Everything may be the proper stuff of fiction, though only some things are the proper stuff for the novel of this or that writer. For instance, for Mrs. Woolf as a writer the lower classes hardly exist; and we have seen that for Hardy as a writer it would have been better if the upper classes had not existed. The novelist must find his own range; if he sees good things impossibly outside it, then he must hope that they may be of use to some other writer. If a good situation or character seem to go to waste, he must remember that there are more situations and characters in life than ever came out of it. He must have faith in two things — the prodigality of life, and the diversity of talent of his brother-artists.

Caveat. While the novelist's 'range' has here been maintained to be more limited than what is ordinarily called his 'experience' nothing has been said of that creative power which transcends what is ordinarily called 'experience'. This does not mean that this power is denied, not even that it is considered ineffable — something might well be said about it at another place and time. But other terminology would probably be required.

NOTES

1. *A Berlin Diary.*
2. *Correspondance*, II, p. 102.
3. cit. Lord David Cecil: *Hardy the Novelist* (1943), pp. 39-40.
4. ibid.
5. Preface to *The Spoils of Poynton.*
6. *Correspondance*, June 1853.
7. ibid.
8. ibid., III, p. 220.
9. loc. cit., p. 13.
10. *Letters of R. L. Stevenson*, September 6th, 1873.
11. *The Letters of D. H. Lawrence* (1934), p. 222: March 1916.
12. *Letters of Katherine Mansfield*, I, p. 233: June 1919.
13. A fine example of the different way in which two writers can react to the same external data is provided by Proust. In a pastiche of the *Journal des Goncourts* he shows Edmond de Goncourt dining with Madame Verdurin: a very different picture from his own of the Salon Verdurin and its 'faithful'. (*Le Temps Retrouvé*, I, pp. 24 ff.)
14. *George Eliot's Life*, by J. W. Cross (1885), II, p. 128.
15. *Journals*, p. 41: January 22nd, 1916.
16. 'Un écrivain peut se mettre sans crainte à un long travail. Que l'intelligence commence son ouvrage, en cours de route surviendront bien assez de chagrins qui se chargeront de le finir. Quant au bonheur, il n'a presqu'une seule utilité, rendre le malheur possible. Il faut que dans le bonheur nous formions de liens bien doux et bien forts de confiance et d'attachement pour que leur rupture nous cause le déchirement si précieux qui s'appelle le malheur. Si l'on n'avait été heureux, ne fût-ce par l'espérance, les malheurs seraient sans cruauté et par conséquent sans fruit.' Proust, *Le Temps Retrouvé*, II, p. 65.
17. *Lions and Shadows.*

18. A 'mystery' play, at one time performed by the players of St. Paul's Covent Garden, showed St. Martha preparing a meal for the disciples, who were likely to come back hungry from witnessing the Crucifixion. That is to go far in 'tea-tabling' events.

19. p. 103.

20. cf. 'In some ways *Between the Acts* is an advance upon *Mrs. Dalloway*, *To the Lighthouse* or *The Waves* because, without loss of depth, it has greater width of interest and greater variety of effect than they have.' Joan Bennett: *Virginia Woolf* (1945), p. 131.

21. loc. cit., p. 130. cf. '(Le livre intérieur) . . . pour sa lecture personne ne pouvait m'aider d'aucune règle, cette lecture consistant en une acte de création où nul ne peut nous suppléer, ni même collaborer avec nous. Aussi combien se détournent de l'écrire, que de tâches n'assume-t-on pas pour éviter celle-là. Chaque événement, que ce fût l'affaire Dreyfus, que ce fût la guerre, avait fourni d'autres excuses aux écrivains pour ne pas déchiffrer ce livre-là; ils voulaient assurer le triomphe du droit, refaire l'unité morale de la nation, n'avaient pas le temps de penser à la littérature . . .' Proust, *Le Temps Retrouvé*, II, pp. 25-6.

22. *Correspondance*, II, pp. 149-50 (1852).

23. cf. the admirable self-denying ordinance of Miss Compton-Burnett (loc. cit.): 'I do not feel that I have any real or organic knowledge of life later than about 1910. I should not write of later times with enough grasp or confidence. I think this is why many writers tend to write of the past. When an age is ended, you see it as it is.'

24. *The Common Reader*, I, 'Modern Fiction'.

CHAPTER III

THE NOVELIST'S VALUES

§ I WE ARE CONCERNED ONLY WITH THE VALUES OF THE 'WRITING SELF'

By 'the novelist' is here intended the writing self; that part of the whole man who is left in the Ivory Tower, with the door shut, writing books. How much of the whole man that will be, will vary from writer to writer. It will depend on how much of his total experience falls within his range as an artist. Our evidence for a writer's 'values', for what he thinks important, can then only validly be drawn from his writings. If we know, for example, from other sources that a writer was in the *maquis*, or that he was with Pétain, we should forget it as a piece of irrelevant gossip. If it was not a part of his experience that fell within his range, it has nothing to do with his work; if it fell within his range as a writer, he will himself tell us what we need to know about it — he cannot avoid it. Therefore any heresy-hunt that proceeds *ab extra*, and not from the examination of a man's works, is, no matter what principles are behind it, as objectionable as the insistence on an artist's 'racial purity'.

§ 2 THE NOVELIST SHOULD BE A HUMANIST: MR. ELIOT'S EIGHT POINTS OF HUMANISM

The novelist's function we have declared to be the conveying to the world in the best chosen language of the most thorough knowledge of human nature, and the happiest delineation of its varieties. If a novelist is to know human nature thoroughly, and to think its varieties worth delineating, then his values must be, fundamentally, humanist values.

Humanism is a vague word — Mr. Eliot says 'necessarily

vague'. For we need vague as well as precise words. The word 'gentleman', for instance, is not philosophical or scientific, but the conception still has its uses. Though we may still dispute about the meaning of the term in detail, yet there is some common agreement about the general meaning. Such a proposition as 'the Prime Minister ought to be a gentleman' would be generally understood, and could be seriously debated.

Of the same order is the statement: 'the novelist ought to be a humanist'. And since the novel itself is not a thing that has ever been very precisely defined, it is clearly improbable that any very precise terms can with propriety be applied to the novelist.

Mr. Eliot has set out eight marks of Humanism:[1] they are not meant to be definitions, they are not meant to be exhaustive. We shall apply them to the novelist and his art.

I. *The function of humanism is not to provide dogmas or philosophical theories . . . it is concerned less with 'reason' than with common sense.*

We have already found Mr. Huxley's egregious young man in *After Many a Summer* complain of the novel that it had 'no co-ordinating philosophy superior to common sense', and Miss Austen's Sir Edward Denham was like-minded with him.

> Sword of Common Sense . . .
> Thine is the service, thine the sport
> This shifty heart of ours to hunt . . .

this is Meredith's address to the Comic Spirit. The novel is certainly one of the time-honoured hunting-grounds of the Comic Spirit, the *Sword of Common Sense*.

And of a work of fiction that provides dogmas or philosophical theories, Proust says simply that it is 'like an object with the price ticket left on'.[2]

II. *Humanism makes for breadth, tolerance, equilibrium and sanity. It operates against fanaticism.*

III. *The world cannot get on without breadth, tolerance and sanity; any more than it can get on without narrowness, bigotry and fanaticism.*

There is undoubtedly a place in Literature, as in Life, for

narrowness, bigotry and fanaticism — bitterness and propaganda can have a place in poetry, as we are often reminded, and Dante was not invariably distinguished by breadth, tolerance, equilibrium and sanity. But it is one thing to do, as poetry and history can do, to pass judgment on a finished action, quite another to show an action taking place, as fiction has to do. The novelist has to get near to or inside his people, to understand not judge them. Satire and heavy irony are things he has to guard against — they are too unsubtle for the work he has to do. Recent research into Miss Austen's methods of work show her controlling her hatred of her characters, suppressing the kind of feeling that expresses itself in satire;[3] and if research into Proust's methods reveals that they were the opposite, some of his later touches were not an improvement.[4]

It would not be easy to find exceptions, great novelists distinguished for narrowness, bigotry and fanaticism. Lawrence might be mentioned, but it is precisely on account of these defects that he fails as a novelist — distorting plot and character in the interests of, and as a result of his anti-humanist values. If he remains a great writer, that is beside the point; for it is certainly not to be maintained that every great writer need be a humanist.

IV. *It is not the business of humanism to refute anything. Its business is to persuade, according to its unformulable axioms of culture and good sense. It does not, for instance, overthrow the arguments of fallacies like Behaviourism: it operates by taste, by sensibility trained by culture. It is critical rather than constructive. It is necessary for the criticism of social life and social theories, political life and political theories. . . .*

V. *Humanism can have no positive theories about philosophy or theology. All that it can ask, in the most tolerant spirit, is: Is this philosophy or religion civilized, or is it not?*

These marks are so obviously true of fiction, that it is hardly necessary to apply them. Novels are nearly always concerned with life as it is or has been lived, and only very exceptionally (and seldom satisfactorily) with life as it might be. And the novelist's only possible comment quâ novelist on a philosophy, a theology or a social theory, is to show its influence on the lives of people who profess it — that is, it can only be critical, not constructive. Thus Dickens in *Hard Times* shows Benthamite Utilitarianism to be uncivilized, thus the novels of Geoffrey Dennis show the religion of the Plymouth brethren to be uncivilized, and those of Jane Austen show early nineteenth-century Anglicanism (touched with Evangelicalism) to be supremely civilized. This is not to affirm that anything about the truth or falsehood of the opinions in question has been demonstrated in those novels.

VI. *There is a type of person whom we call the Humanist, for whom Humanism, is enough. This type is valuable.*

It is perhaps unlikely that the novelist will often belong to this type. 'The pitfall for such an author is obvious,' Mr. Forster has written. 'It is the Palace of Art, it is that bottomless chasm of dullness which pretends to be a palace, all glorious with corridors and domes, but which is really a dreadful hole into which the unwary aesthete may tumble, to be seen no more.'[5] There have, however, been novelists of this type, and Mr. Forster goes on to claim that Virginia Woolf was such a one, who have nevertheless escaped this pitfall.

VII. *Humanism is valuable* (a) *by itself, in the 'pure humanist', who will not set up humanism as a substitute for philosophy and religion, and* (b) *as a mediating and corrective ingredient in a positive civilization founded on definite belief.*

As an example of the humanist who accepts a definite system of belief, which he is able to reconcile with humanist standards, Mr. Eliot cites the great Catholic writer, Baron Friedrich von Hügel. Mr. Eliot himself is probably the most distinguished living humanist of this type.

The novelist, naturally, may belong to either type, but if he accepts a definite system of belief, then it must be a system or belief in itself not incompatible with humanist standards, and he must not accept it with an anti-humanist fanaticism — an attitude which can, unhappily, be applied to systems of belief which do not require it, and which are not in themselves opposed to humanism.

Thus a novelist may be Protestant, Catholic, agnostic or atheist; he may be imperialist, pacifist, conservative, liberal or socialist, independent or apolitical. He may be any of these things with complete conviction — a conviction firm enough for him to think all other points of view mistaken. But he may not have an angry conviction. He must be able to understand and to sympathize with views he does not share. He must not think that everyone who differs from him is ill-informed, unintelligent, or acting in bad faith.

Whether a Marxist or a Fascist can be a Humanist may be doubted, and therefore it may be doubted whether tolerable novels can be written by a Marxist or a Fascist. But it would be altogether a wrong and unhumane procedure to say that such a man was a Marxist or Fascist, and therefore *a priori* could not write tolerable novels. We must look at the books, not at the party labels. If we find that, after all, a Marxist or Fascist has managed to be a Humanist, we shall, if we are Humanists, be inclined to rejoice at the fact — rather than to lament that a Humanist could be a Marxist or a Fascist. Although the careful toeing of a party-line does not make for humanism, it is quite certain that 'near-Marxists' and 'near-Fascists' may be very good Humanists indeed.

In looking at a novelist's belief, then, we should not greatly trouble ourselves about what external system, if any, he accepts. We should trouble ourselves rather about the disposition with which he accepts it. We should inquire whether his private and personal values are humane or no. And, holding the eminently humanist view that there are good men in every camp, we should ask whether the novelist is one of those good men, in whatever camp he may be found. That is, of course, we should ask if his 'writing self' is a good and valuable self. And, we are to remember, the 'writing self' may differ in important respects from the self that votes or goes to church — only the evidence of the written word is valid here.

The understanding of these so simple principles would save a world of heresy-hunting and of pseudo-criticism. It would prevent the asking of such unreal questions as: 'Should the novelist concern himself with contemporary social problems?'

It may be laid down that to all such questions, if they begin *should*, the answer is *No*; if they begin *may*, the answer is *Yes*. Even when (which is rare) they are couched in the most rudimentary form which has any claim to be an intelligent question, e.g.: 'in what circumstances may the novelist concern himself with contemporary social problems?' — the answer is so simple that it can be stated in a few words: 'if they lie within his range, if he looks at them as a humanist, and if he treats them as a novelist — that is, in terms of character in action.'

Such questions ought not to trouble a creative writer, though their parrot-like reiteration is bound to sink into his consciousness, and there can be little doubt that harm has been done to literature in this way. For example, the absurd question: 'ought literature to have a social message?' may ring like an advertisement slogan in a writer's ears till he comes to think that it ought, and that when writing he ought to try to put such a message in — oblivious of the fact that a 'message' is something that the reader gets out of a book, not something that the writer puts into it.

VIII. *Humanism, finally, is valid for a very small minority of individuals. But it is culture, not any subscription to a common programme or platform which binds these individuals together. Such an 'intellectual aristocracy' has not the economic bonds which unite the individuals of an 'aristocracy of birth'.*

To this aristocracy we have a right to demand that any novelist or any critic who is to be taken seriously shall belong. A novelist who insists too much upon the external system of belief which he accepts, a critic who insists too much upon the external system of belief accepted by an author, are being vulgar; they are putting their aristocracy in doubt. It is on their common humanism that humanists meet.

Therefore, for example, a Catholic may delight in Samuel

Butler, and hold Belloc and Chesterton in abhorrence — and this does not mean that he is not in agreement with Belloc and Chesterton over things which he regards of infinitely more importance than the nausea with which their style affects him. For it is Humanism, rather than doctrine that will (if we are Humanists) decide what books we read. The same principles will to some extent determine who are our friends; and in certain circumstances our actions may be determined by them in a crisis. A 'pure humanist' will choose to die with his friends, rather than for this or that cause.

Catholic and Socialist critics have claimed that for a novelist it is a positive advantage to be, respectively, a Catholic or a Socialist. For, they say, our view of the world is the right one, and if you look at the world from the right point of view, then you will see everything in its proper place, including those things which are the subjects of fiction.

This looks reasonable upon the face of it. But if we ask ourselves if it would help a botanist, quâ botanist, if he were a Catholic or a Socialist, we shall see at once that that would be absurd. The novelist is concerned, like the botanist, with particular manifestations of life, for which he requires very sharp eyes, and not with life in general. The only advantage of a true belief about Life in general to a novelist would be negative: it would protect him from false belief. Thus a Catholic novelist is protected from Behaviourism — a belief which would make it difficult for him to regard the particular manifestations of life, which are his subject-matter, as a novelist should.

However, any general philosophy of life, true or false, applied deductively by a novelist to particular instances would be almost certain to have a fatal effect upon his art. Whether he saw Original Sin everywhere, or the Oedipus Complex, the results would be equally disastrous. This is not to affirm that they are not everywhere.

§ 3 A NINTH POINT: THE PROPER VIRTUES OF THE NOVELIST

To Mr. Eliot's eight marks of Humanism, we might add a ninth. If Humanism makes for breadth, tolerance, equilibrium and sanity, then the humanist virtues will be Justice, and its better part, Mercy.

To persons gifted or cursed with the abnormal Sensibility which is associated with the man of letters, the virtues of temperance, fortitude and prudence may well be difficult; they may have peculiarly strong temptations against them. There have been excellent writers who have not been prudent, temperate or brave. Fortitude, in particular, is so easy to practise on paper that it can hardly be attributed to the writing self at all. And it is with the writing self, not the whole man, that we are concerned. How good or bad the whole man is does not matter to the critic or the reader, if the vices have been kept out of the writing self; and there have been very bad men who have kept their writing selves clean.[6]

The virtues of Justice and Mercy, however, are as hard to practise on paper as anywhere else. They are the specific virtues of the critic, and without them he has no claim to that title; and they are of almost equal importance to the novelist.

The important thing to discover about the novelist is not chiefly what characters he thinks good, but rather what characters he thinks 'nice' — in spite of Henry Tilney, this vague word is yet the best for what is in part, but by no means entirely, a moral value. We are not satisfied with a nice character unless he embodies some degree of Mercy and Justice — Justice being understood to include honesty with oneself as well as with other people.

It might be thought that this is a modern prejudice. 'For about a hundred years,' writes Mr. C. S. Lewis, 'we have so concentrated on one of the virtues — "kindness" or mercy — that most of us do not feel anything except kindness to be really good or anything but cruelty to be really bad. Such lop-sided ethical developments are not uncommon, and other ages too have had their pet virtues and curious insensibilities.'[7]

Nevertheless, while we agree with Mr. Lewis that the possessors of other virtues have in other times been more esteemed for goodness than the just or the merciful, we may yet claim some degree of catholicity for the view that they are especially 'nice' — as something *quod semper, quod usque, quod ab omnibus receptum est*. There can be no attempt here to prove this point, but one might mention, for example, how *nice* some people are in the *Inferno* (e.g. Brunetto Latini), and how nice Dante evidently thought them; yet they could not be good, or they would not be there. They are never people who have sinned against Mercy.

No doubt it would be a grave fault in a novelist to belittle Prudence, Temperance or Fortitude in any way, or ever to represent them in themselves as less than good; though they well might form part of extremely unattractive characters — the same would be true of Justice dissociated from Mercy.[8] But, if one may say so without irreverence, the blessing pronounced upon the Merciful appears to have effect in the natural as well as in the supernatural order, and in Letters as well as Life — they shall obtain mercy. It would be hard to find a conspicuously merciful person, in Life or Letters, whom one could regard as a disagreeable character. One could not indeed make a similar judgment about any other virtue.

§ 4 THE DETACHMENT OF THE NOVELIST

There is an argument against the Humanism of the novelist (or indeed of any writer) which is often and noisily put forward. It should therefore be answered, though it is not in fact very intelligent.

It is objected that in 'these critical times' civilization is in danger, and that there is no time for tolerance or sanity. The novelist, like everyone else, must fight.

Now if people who said this meant that in a moment of crisis the whole man (of which the writing self is a part) may be required in the general interest to engage in some work of public importance, no one could well object. If Rome were burning, the novelist, like everyone else, might be needed to fill buckets of water. But his 'writing self' cannot fill buckets of water, and must resist all efforts at mobilization. One may be too busy filling buckets of water to have time to write, but if one manages to go on writing (as writers generally do) it will not be any part of one's duty to write against the fire.

This popular error is due to several causes. In the first place an exaggerated reaction against the doctrine of 'Art for Art's sake' has morbidly affected some writers, so that they are anxious at any moment to justify their work on practical grounds. Next, in wartime everyone becomes so anxious to do his 'bit', or to prove that he is doing it, and to see that his neighbour is doing the like, that the 'writing self' has not been exempted — has not been understood to be essentially non-belligerent.

Of course any dangers to civilization and to humanist values that may arise, are best combatted by the novelist if he continues to affirm those values in his quiet, unfanatical way. On a short time view, his worst danger is not the Enemy (whoever that may happen to be) but those worthy people who, on the highest grounds, and with the motive of preserving civilization, attack that little part of civilization which is the equilibrium and sanity of the writer. On a long time view, it would probably be hard to find any cultivated person who sincerely believed that civilization has at any time since the renaissance been in danger of more than a temporary eclipse or setback. Any historian is likely to have handled enough books that have at one time or another been condemned to be burnt, to laugh at any threatened burning of books. Anyone who has learnt Latin has learnt that 'captive Greece tamed her fierce victor', and knows that civilization is always an incomparably more dangerous enemy to barbarism than the barbarians can be to civilization.

The acceptance of these simple, even platitudinous, axioms

would put an end to the abuse of such words as 'Escapism' — which have had their day. And the 'contemporary subject' would not be allowed to exercise the same tyranny over the short story that the 'poetical subject' exercised over the lyric at the beginning of this century. Both tyrannies are death to creative writing, and *Folios of New Writing*, now not so new, have joined in the lumber-room *Poems of To-day*, whose day has become the day before yesterday.

It has to be remembered that a writer's is a contemplative, not an active vocation. 'A man who has set up as an artist', says Flaubert, 'has not the right to live as others.'⁹ This does not mean indifference to the life of the world outside the Ivory Tower; it does mean detachment from it. 'I am prepared', says Conrad, 'to put up serenely with the insignificance which attaches to persons who are not meddlesome in some way or other. But resignation is not indifference. I would not like to be left standing as a mere spectator on the bank of the great stream carrying onward so many lives. I would fain claim for myself the faculty of so much insight as can be expressed in a voice of sympathy and compassion.'¹⁰

The contemplative writer serves the world in detachment from it, just as in his different and harder way the contemplative religious serves the world. And the writer also can offer his pains for the world, and they are no mean pains. Among minor pin-pricks, not worthy to be mentioned beside the pains of creation, are the pushes and nudges he receives from people who try to disturb his essential equilibrium and sanity, which they miscall complacency and indifference.

The writer is in no way severed from the world, nor is his art an abstract skill. Therefore when Mr. F. L. Lucas says: 'To ignore the values of real life in judging the values of literature, to talk as if art were a sublime bag of tricks, to care nothing whether a book is sordid, or whimpering, or cruel, is a new *trahison des clercs*',¹¹ we may agree with him — except that there is nothing new about it — little as we may agree with his applications of this point of view. He continues: 'This does not mean returning to the prejudices of 1850 and screaming at *Jane Eyre* as immoral; the trouble with such judges was not that they treated literature as bearing on life, but that their view of life happened to be stupid.' We should also add that their view of the way in which literature bore on life was also stupid; it was illiberal, not humane.

§5 THE FOREGOING PRINCIPLES APPLIED: A BRIEF EXAMEN OF MR. E. M. FORSTER'S NOVELS

It is not the purpose of this chapter to prove or to refute anything that moral philosophers or social theorists may have to say about the place of the novelist in the world, and the duties of his place. Its method is that of persuasion rather than proof. Its purpose is in part casuistical (in the good and proper use of that word), aiming to quiet consciences of general readers, critics, or writers, that have been inflamed by much contemporary journalism and conversation. And though it would be an intolerable impertinence to offer a writer advice about the choice of an outlook on life, it is not at all improper to suggest that a novelist may examine himself (and that his critics and readers may examine him), whether he holds his outlook on life (whatever it may be) with the tolerance and sanity proper to a humanist. If he is temperamentally a bigot, then his vocation as a novelist may be questioned.

Moreover a right understanding of what a novelist's values should be has a practical value in criticism. Let us illustrate this point by applying the foregoing principles to the work of a given writer. We will make a brief examen of some early works of Mr. E. M. Forster.

The values which Mr. Forster defends, when they are his main subject, are always those of culture and civilization. Monteriano, with its architectural and natural beauty, and the gay and natural life of its inhabitants, is defended against the drab, suburban conventionality of Sawston — *a land of lobelias and of tennis flannels*. Cambridge, with its sweetness and light, provides a standard for the condemnation of the minor public school at Sawston, and the sham Roman virtues that it inculcates. The wisdom of the Schlegels about personal relations, and their love of the Arts, shows up the 'outer world' of the Wilcoxes, behind all their 'telegrams and anger', as one of 'panic and emptiness'. Aziz, with his imaginative enthusiasm for the great Mogul past, Professor Godbole, with his Hindu mysticism, even Miss Quested, with her earnest attempts at intellectual honesty, all stand for something higher than the English Club at Chandrapore, with its purely conventional decencies and loyalties — which are valuable as far as they go, but which are shown not to stand the test of a real crisis.

Mr. Forster is a Humanist, we see clearly from his fiction, and he has made the fact abundantly clear in his other writing. If we apply the 'cabman's test' to his novels, opening them at random and examining a single page here or there, we are certain to discover an exquisite sensibility at work, and to hear a beautiful, gentle, wise, truthful and virtuous voice speaking.

It is a truthful, that is a sincere voice that is speaking; but though we never doubt the sincerity, we may at times have grave doubts about the truth of what is said. It is the maintenance of several minor heresies (from the humanist point of view) that detracts from the total value of some of the earlier of Mr. Forster's novels. The elucidation of these heresies — which critics appear to have neglected — may help us to see why these books, though in many ways so beautiful, are so unsatisfactory in their total effect.

The first false doctrine may be called the doctrine of the Great Refusal.

Rickie Elliot in *The Longest Journey* sins against truth, by entangling himself with his wife and his brother-in-law, and by becoming involved in their shiftiness and false standards; one sin leads to another, until his character is so warped that only a violent break could save him. This part of the moral tale is true and convincing.

But he also sins against kindness; he commits a small, though an extremely deliberate sin. He has learned that Stephen (a 'Rough Diamond' or 'Noble Savage') is his illegitimate half-brother, and he is disgusted. But Stephen seems in an odd way to be important to him, though he does not like him.

He says to Agnes, his wife: 'It seems to me that here and there in life we meet with a person or incident that is symbolical. It is nothing in itself, yet for the moment it stands for some eternal principle. We have accepted it, at whatever cost, and we have accepted life. But if we are frightened and reject it, the moment, so to speak, passes; the symbol is never offered again.'

Stephen calls under Rickie's window three times — Rickie hesitates, is held back by Agnes, and does not reply to his call. We are meant, no doubt, to think of another three-fold denial. This time, however, there is no saving cock-crow. It is the beginning of Rickie's spiritual death. Two years later he confesses it to Stephen, adding: 'Ever since then I have taken the world at second-hand. I have bothered less and less to look it in the face — until not only you, but everyone else has turned unreal.' Stephen says nothing to this, and one cannot imagine that he could have understood a word of it.

This is not to attack the psychology of the book. A rather feeble character like Rickie, and one for whom the imagination took the foremost place, and not the intellect, if he had made unto himself a symbol, and had then out of cowardice rejected it, might not improbably have a general physical and spiritual breakdown afterwards.

What is wrong is the morality of the book. Mr. Forster makes it clear that he is handing out to Rickie what be believes to be suitable punishment. Yet we cannot really think that Rickie has done anything so terrible as to deserve his spiritual hell. He has been rather weak, but unless (as it is to be feared Mr. Forster has) we also make a fetish of the Noble Savage, we cannot feel a turning-away from him, if slightly unkind, to be deeply wicked. The doctrine of the Noble Savage, the second heresy we shall speak of, must however be isolated, and reserved for a later attack.

The notion of a Great Refusal — of a life spiritually laid waste by a very small sin of omission — is, if we look at it, more stupid and vindictive than the crudest medieval or puritan view of Hell. It is contrary to traditional moral philosophy, in which virtue is a good habit, not destroyed, though possibly rendered more difficult, by the commission of a bad act. If it is true in any psychology, it can only be in the psychology of morbid states. A healthy, adult soul can digest a certain amount of evil, even of its own evil, without being permanently the worse. Though Christian theology teaches that grace can be destroyed in the soul by a single sin, yet it requires such a sin to be of much more moment than poor Rickie's, and provides means for the restoration of grace.

The notion of the Great Refusal is neither sensible nor civilized: it looks like a superstitious and sentimental perversion of a religious doctrine, of the kind one sometimes encounters in the work of writers who neither have a definite system of belief, nor find it easy to get on without one. A nineteenth-century tract-writer, who might have shown a small sin like this of Rickie's leading to lies, and on to worse sins, would be setting forth a more convincing morality than that of this part of *The Longest Journey* — and such has been Mr. Forster's own method with Rickie's decline from truth. But this one rejection of Stephen has been allowed to cut Rickie off from 'Life' — 'Life', presumably, being a vague and muddled secular equivalent of sanctifying grace.

But there is worse to come. In *A Room with a View* the heroine, Lucy, is aware that she is in love with George (like Stephen, he is something of a Noble Savage). She honestly breaks her engagement to another man, but she is determined (for many excellent reasons) to resist her love for George. This is how Mr. Forster puts it: 'Love felt and returned, Love which our bodies exact and our hearts have transfigured, Love which is the most real thing that we shall ever meet, reappeared now as the world's worst enemy, and she must stifle it.' As if this were not how Love often makes his appearance.

Lucy, in short, intends to make the Great Refusal, in which she is backed up by her cousin Charlotte. And Mr. Forster takes it very tragically.

'It did not do to think, nor, for the matter of that, to feel. She gave up trying to understand herself, and joined the vast armies of the benighted, who follow neither the heart nor the brain, and march to their destiny by catchwords. The armies are full of pleasant and pious folk. But they have yielded to the only enemy that matters — the enemy within. They have sinned against passion and truth, and vain will be their strife after virtue. As the years pass, they are censured. Their pleasantry and their piety show cracks, their wit becomes cynicism, their unselfishness hypocrisy; they feel and produce discomfort wherever they go. They have sinned against Eros and against Pallas Athene, and not by any heavenly intervention, but by the ordinary course of nature, those allied deities will be avenged.'

Whatever spiritual truth there may be behind the doctrine of the Great Refusal — for, like every other heresy it contains some truth — it is here a good deal overstated. Lucy has decided to reject the purely physical advances of a very ineligible young man — no friendship has had opportunity to spring up between them. Mr. Forster lets the reader know that George was in fact the right man for Lucy, but she herself had no way of knowing it. Their bodies might exact love, but their hearts had not yet transfigured it. And even if Love is the most real thing we shall ever meet — one wonders why it should be more 'real' than any other experience, but let that pass — Lucy, who was young and attractive, might well have met it again and again, if she had rejected it upon this occasion. Mr. Forster is being harder than God or Life would have been to Lucy — he wants to deny her another chance. The 'night' is to receive her, as it received Charlotte thirty years before. Even if Lucy must follow Charlotte's example, rejecting love, and retiring to Tunbridge Wells, there are many worse ways of managing one's life.

Mr. Forster is hard on Lucy, he is hard on Rickie, because of an inordinate value which he sets upon Stephen and George. He believes in the Noble Savage, and in Passion.

To some extent, of course, we all do. We have had the happiness to know 'Noble Savages' or 'Nature's Gentlemen' — people who by native goodness judge and act wisely and rightly and graciously, where less favoured people have to be guided by thought and training. We ought to love and respect their natural wisdom and goodness, as we ought to love and respect wisdom and goodness wherever they occur. And over-sophisticated persons who fail to appreciate the Noble Savage are to be pitied. Possibly Mr. Forster wanted to give the Noble Savage a fair deal in Letters; he may have thought that he had there been neglected. This is a piece of justice that does not at all cry out to be done. The 'Noble Savage' has a fine time in Life, for which he is admirably adapted — if Letters should do him less than justice, he has no right to complain.

Intellectual persons are often less beautiful than the Noble Savage — at all events while he is young, for in old age they sometimes get their own back on him. They tend to stoop, to be too thin or too fat, or both at once, and in the wrong places. They are bad at doing things which he does superbly — such as riding a horse or handling a boat. They are often full of jealousy and dislike for each other. They are apt to lack the noble virtue of Fortitude — particularly in its more dashing form.[12] There-fore it is a great temptation to intellectual persons to fall in love with the Noble Savage, and to exalt him and his passions over people of their own sort, and their thoughts and feelings.

If this is carried too far, and the Savage is exalted beyond his due, intuition and instinct are made of more account than the intellect — it is a very bad form of the *trahison des clercs*. It is, in subtle disguise, the very sin of Sawston, which Mr. Forster has in its place condemned, 'the contempt for the intellect'. Stephen as much as Agnes, cannot be infinitely over-estimated without 'the lie in the soul'.

Idolatrous worship of the Noble Savage is a sin that generally brings its own punishment with it. Mr. Forster has not escaped.

This heresy involves him, as it nearly always involves writers who hold it, in an artistic fault. The Noble Savage is extremely hard to portray convincingly, and generally comes into fiction with his nobility left behind. It is no good an author saying he is noble, as he might say that his heroine is beautiful; we withhold our respect from him, unless he is convincingly worthy of our respect. George in *A Room with a View*, and Stephen in *The Longest Journey*, do not really convince; therefore any emotional argument based on their nobility falls to the ground.

These two departures from Humanist values, these doctrines of the Great Refusal, and of the Noble Savage, heresies from the point of view of culture, sanity and common sense, mar some of Mr. Forster's early work, for all the wise Humanism of his considered attitude.

NOTES

1. *Second Thoughts on Humanism.*
2. *Le Temps Retrouvé*, II, p. 29.
3. Recent essays in *Scrutiny* by Q. D. Leavis, particularly '*Lady Susan*' into '*Mansfield Park*' (Oct. 1941).
4. Albert Feuillerat: *Comment Marcel Proust a-t-il composé son roman?* Esp. for the characters of Françoise and of Madame de Marsantes.
5. Rede lecture, *Virginia Woolf*, p. 9.
6. 'That writer's books you tell me about, the books the virtuous in England will not read because his private life was disgraceful, beautiful books, you say, into which went his best, in which his spirit showed how bright it was, how he had kept it apart and clean, I shall get them all and read them all. No sinner, cursed with a body at variance with his soul and able in spite of it to hear the music of heaven and give it exquisite expression, shall ever again be identified by me with what at such great pains he has kept white. I know at least three German writers to whom the same thing has happened, men who live badly and write nobly. My heart goes out to them. I think of them, lame and handicapped, leading their muse by the hand with anxious care so that her shining feet, set among the grass and daisies along the roadside, shall not be dimmed by the foulness through which

they themselves are splashing.' 'Elizabeth': *Fräulein Schmidt and Mr. Anstruther,* XLVII.

7. *The Problem of Pain,* pp. 43-4.
8. This is misunderstood by those persons who accuse Lytton Strachey e.g. of belittling the humanitarianism and courage of Florence Nightingale, to which he extends full admiration, because he shows them coexisting (as they did) with other less amiable traits of character.
9. *Correspondance,* August 28th, 1876.
10. *A Personal Record:* 'A Familiar Preface'.
11. *Critical thoughts in Critical Days* (P.E.N. Books), p. 53. Against this nasty, little pamphlet, whose author lacks the effrontery to blame inter-war literature for the losing of the Peace and for the defeat of France, but affirms that *tout se tient,* one should set the sanity of M. André Gide: '*Il me paraît aussi absurde d'incriminer notre littérature au sujet de notre défaite qu'il l'eût été de la féliciter en 1918, lorsque nous avions la victoire . . .*' But Mr. Lucas has received condign execution at the hands of Sir Osbert Sitwell in *A Letter to my Son.*
12. We are not to deny to any writer some measure of endurance: without it he could not finish writing a book. Whereas some people lack the endurance even to finish reading a book. This point might have been given more consideration by such writers as Mr. C. S. Lewis, who seek to put down the artist from his place and to exalt the 'little man' — a dreary object of worship. In some rare cases the writer's endurance attains the degree of heroism. See Appendix I: the examples of heroism there may even be a little frightening to those who are only called to be conscientious, minor writers. So those who are only called to be everyday Christians may sometimes be frightened when they read the lives of the Saints. Moreover, the novelist requires the fortitude to see life steadily, even if he is not obliged to see it whole: like the governess in *The Turn of the Screw* (see Appendix II) he needs the 'indispensable little note of courage, without which he wouldn't have had his data'.

CHAPTER IV

THE MAKING OF PLOT

§1 PLOT ONLY ARTIFICIALLY SEPARABLE FROM CHARACTER

Any writer of fiction will tell you that he is commonly asked this question: 'Which do you think of first, the characters or the plot?' It is a very banal question, and it generally makes writers very angry. It is an ignorant question, and yet it has in it something of the malice of fools. It is ignorant, because with a little thought anyone could realize that characters and plot are only artificially separable. As Henry James says: 'Character, in any sense in which we can get at it, is action, and action is plot, and any plot which hangs together, even if it pretend to interest us only in the fashion of a Chinese puzzle, plays upon our emotion, our suspense, by means of personal references. We care for people only in proportion as we know what people are.'[1] In a perfect novel interesting characters are displayed in a coherent and well-shaped action, and probably they have grown together in the author's mind. But very often a situation or a character has been what the novelist started from; he has had to look for characters, or he has had to look for a story. Perhaps he is not quite satisfied with his final union of story and people, and the questioner has put a finger on a sore place.

§2 THE EXPANSION OF A SITUATION: 'THE SPOILS OF POYNTON'

Henry James himself nearly always began with plot, and the germ or seed of the plot he picked up in some way from life, by observation or hearsay. 'Such is the interesting truth', he writes, 'about the stray suggestion, the wandering word, the vague echo, at touch of which the novelist's imagination winces as at the prick of some sharp point; its virtue is all in its needle-like quality, the power to penetrate as finely as possible . . . one's subject is in the merest grain, the speck of truth, of beauty, of reality, scarce visible to the common eye.'[2] Life, so to speak gave Henry James a pin-prick, and injected a germ, and this germ was nearly always the germ of a story. Heine said that out of his great sorrows he made his little songs: *Aus meinen grossen Schmerzen mach' ich die kleinen Lieder.* Henry James made his great novels out of little scraps of other people's talk.

Changing his metaphor, he tells us: 'Most of the stories straining to shape under my hand have sprung from a single small seed, a seed as minute and windblown as that casual hint for *The Spoils of Poynton* dropped unwitting by my neighbour, a mere floating particle in the stream of talk.'[3]

His neighbour at a dinner-party, in the course of conversation, gave him the subject of that wonderful novel. This is how he narrates it, and it is no doubt almost an exact reproduction of the written or mental note which he made after the dinner-party. 'A good lady in the north, always well looked on, was at daggers drawn with her only son, ever hitherto exemplary, over the ownership of the valuable furniture of a fine old house just accruing to the young man by his father's death.'[4]

This little anecdote gave Henry James what in another place he speaks of as 'a jog of fond Fancy's elbow'.[5]

Creation is a mysterious process, perhaps, as Mrs. Wharton suggested, ineffable like the mystic's experience, and only vaguely to be conveyed, by analogy. Therefore it is necessary to be patient with all the metaphors which are used about it. The fact that Henry James uses so many is due to his closer approach than that of any other man to the description of the indescribable.

He tells us that he wished to stop the lady's story then and there; he had received enough. She went on telling it, and it was full of details that were no use to him. In the sequel he saw 'clumsy life again at her stupid work'. For life 'has no direct sense whatever for the subject and is capable, luckily for us, of nothing but splendid waste . . .'[6] Life, that is, is full of subjects, but with no idea how to treat them.

Man is always ready to recreate God in his own image: the novelist is no exception. He is apt to see the Almighty as a novelist, author of a grandiose *Comédie Humaine* — an enormously vital and creative novelist, but clumsy, and with no idea of construction. Some few characters show an observable pattern in their lives, but most do not. He is like Balzac, or Dickens, or Proust — an immense genius, but careless. The only carelessness, almost, that He does not commit is that of Thackeray in *The Newcomes* — He does not forget when characters have died. When we have died we are dead, and not liable to appear again a few chapters ahead. As Flaubert said, He mixes His genres: tragedy and comedy are inextricably muddled up in life.

A novelist like Henry James, with a love of architecture, will be inclined to extract passages from this vast *Comédie Humaine*, and to treat them in his own way, with more artistry. And because he sees life itself as a huge work of fiction, and his own fiction as a form of life, he can feel that an historical fact is not 'what really happened'. What really happened was what Art demanded should have happened.

Therefore to Henry James the beautiful implications evolved in his own mind were of a higher reality than the vulgar quarrel between mother and son that his neighbour at dinner told him about. *The Spoils of Poynton* tells us what really occurred: it is the perfect expansion of a situation.

Starting as he did, with a single situation, Henry James had to discover what characters could have brought such a situation about, and were best fitted to bring out its beautiful implications. Two characters were given in the situation: 'the good lady in the north, always well looked on', had presumably some special claim to the furniture, therefore (he decided) she had originally collected it, therefore she must be extremely clever, and must have a passion for beautiful things. The only son, 'ever hitherto exemplary' must be a right-feeling gentleman;

otherwise the quarrel over possessions with his mother would be merely sordid and uninteresting. And because Henry James intended developments of extreme subtlety, he needed a character to appreciate the finer points, which would be lost on the mother, who stood mainly for cleverness, and on the son, who stood for average good behaviour. Therefore the mother was given as a confidant an exquisite being, rather cruelly named by her creator Fleda Vetch, who stood for the most refined intelligence, and the most sensitive honour. Acting as go-between for mother and son, Fleda transfigures their ugly disputes by the beauty of her personality. Moreover she and the son fall in love, which very much contributes to the distress of the story.

But unfortunately cleverness, right-feeling, sensitiveness and honour are on the whole static qualities; a dynamic character was needed to precipitate Action. Will initiates Action, therefore the son was given a fiancée embodying brute will-power, and she made the story go.

Thus the functions of the four chief characters were dictated by the story — but they are four living people, not dressed-up abstractions, and in their turn they have taken over the working out of the story into their own hands and have (incidentally) brought it to the saddest ending in English fiction.

It all looks so simple, the architecturally built plot, the interesting characters, that for a moment we may be tempted to believe that we ourselves could have done what Henry James did with his material. We could not. Probably we should not even have thought twice about the little anecdote, if it had been told to us.

'The power that recognizes the fruitful idea and seizes it, is a thing apart,' wrote Percy Lubbock. 'For this reason we judge the novelist's eye for a subject to be his cardinal gift.'[7] Henry James had this gift eminently, and it is the singleness of subject in his most successful plots that gives them a simplicity underlying all their subtlety; and that is why they look as if they had been easy to think of. On the other hand a really ungainly plot, like that of *The Return of the Native*, looks as if it had been very difficult to think of. Would, as Dr. Johnson might have said, it had been impossible!

§3 THE NOVELIST'S PERVERSITY

Using Henry James's own word, we have spoken of the implications in the story of *The Spoils of Poynton* as 'beautiful' — a story full of intrigue, jealousy and acquisitiveness. Clearly this is not what ordinary people mean when they speak of situations or characters as beautiful; there is no connection here with moral beauty. However, as to a portrait painter a merely pretty face may present no interest, but an old woman such as Rembrandt painted may serve him as a model for the beauty he wishes to express — so moral ugliness, baseness of character, or a thoroughly unrighteous state of affairs may make a novelist exclaim: 'how beautiful!' This sometimes annoys other people very much, and they think him perverse because he is not so much shocked as they are. It is not, however, that he is blind to moral turpitude or social injustice — it is that if he looks at a situation, as a novelist, he is most concerned with the complications lurking in it, and he is fascinated by the side-lights that it gives him upon human life. The broad, full-face meaning of the situation may matter less to him. And there is no reason why he should be condemned for looking at life aesthetically, not ethically or politically. No sane person would expect a landscape artist to be thinking of the crops or the farmers every time he looked at the weather.

And to some extent, of course, the novelist really is perverse: it may be doubted if anyone would trouble to write if there were nothing at all wrong with him.

A perfect world would provide no copy, and it is much to be doubted whether a perfect man could write readable novels even about this world we live in. Literature is one of the happier consequences of the Fall of Man, and those of us who do not believe in human progress may find this thought a consolation

76

when, like Camilla in *Great Expectations*, we wake up in the night.

The perversity of the novelist will generally be found to contain a streak of cruelty, and it will need all his humanistic reverence for mercy and justice to keep it from over-development — it would be difficult to name a good novelist who is not in some way cruel. Henry James, gloating over the kind of evil situation which inspired *The Spoils of Poynton* is such an instance. And as the novelist, like anyone else, does not take in experience passively, but transmutes it from the first moment into something that he can assimilate, very odd things may happen to the germs or seeds of plot that observation or hearsay give him.

§4 THE GENESIS OF AN EPISODE:
'DU CÔTÉ DE MONTJOUVAIN'

The best example of the genesis of an episode, due to the perversity of a novelist, is one that is both famous and extremely unpleasant. It is that story which, if we extract it out of the immense novel of Proust, we may find it convenient to label with a name of its own. Let us call it 'Du Côté de Montjouvain'.

Montjouvain was situated *du côté de chez Swann*; to reach it, one turned off the road somewhere between Combray and Méséglise. It had been the residence of M. Vinteuil, the music teacher, and after his death it belonged to his daughter. One evening the narrator, hidden in the shrubbery, witnessed the loves of Mademoiselle Vinteuil and her friend. Mademoiselle Vinteuil, as a preliminary preparation, had put her father's photograph in a prominent position; then by repeated remarks such as: 'what would he say if he could see us now?' she incited her friend to insult him, and to spit upon his photograph. This was apparently part of the ritual of their love-making. To the reader, who remembers M. Vinteuil's former pride in his daughter, and the pain her conduct subsequently gave him, and his broken life and ambitions, and great musical genius, the scene is one of almost diabolic cruelty. It is the more unbearable because we know that all the time Mademoiselle Vinteuil profoundly loved her father; we shall see later the proof she gave of it.

By great good fortune we know how Proust came to conceive this incident. The Duchesse de Clermont-Tonnerre has told us, in her recollections of Marcel Proust, the innocent little story which was the origin of this tale of horror.

A man, though devoted to his wife and child, had a mistress. Such was his devotion to his wife and child that he never stopped talking about them when he visited her. She got tired of this, and said she never wanted to hear again about 'my wife' and 'my child'. 'What am I to call them, then?' asked her lover. She answered pettishly: 'The monster, and the little monster.'

In Proust's memory this story became deformed into one where a man perversely delighted to call his wife and child, whom he really loved, by abusive names, when he was making love with his mistress. By easy transitions from this state, and rendered into terms of Lesbianism, it ended up in the horrible incident *du Côté de Montjouvain*.

Here we see raw material passing through a novelist's mind, and perhaps not a very nice mind. However it was the mind of one of the greatest men of this century, and therefore a little more ought to be said. If Proust degraded Mademoiselle Vinteuil to the depths, yet he also raised her. She and her friend later, in penitence for what they had made Vinteuil suffer in his lifetime, gave him an immortality after death by the most devoted puzzling out from scraps of manuscript, and the most careful editing of his great septet, in comparison with which, we are told, even his great sonata, whose unheard melodies haunt us all through Proust's novel, was merely banal.[8]

This is only one of the many stories in *A la Recherche du Temps Perdu* which show that it is more a Divine than a Human Comedy. This is often lost sight of because there is so much and such fearful Inferno, and because so many readers lose their way and never get to the end, or are tired when they get there. And it is a great seer who is our guide.

The novelist is not one who delights to see the best in everybody. He is, on the contrary, particularly fond of Crime. In Murder, for instance, human passions are laid extraordinarily bare, and the principal character, at least, acts with a decision and a violence that the novelist seldom ventures to give to one of his own creatures. Moreover, there is often a very good story. Turn the pages of *Who's Who* and you will find that, of those novelists who have the bad taste to give personal details about themselves, many name Criminology as one of their hobbies. Henry James himself (though indeed in a private letter) wrote almost lyrically about the great poisoner, Madeleine Smith. Dickens took the greatest interest in Wainewright (whom he had been privileged to meet), and also in Professor Webster. Although out of a sense of duty a novelist may read the front pages of his newspaper, his natural inclination is to the *faits divers*.

M. André Gide for years collected reports of crimes from the newspapers: two cases haunted him, stirred in his mind, and gave him no rest until he had made a plot that linked them together. We have seen in the incident at Montjouvain how the genesis of an episode has occurred in a novelist's mind; in *The Spoils of Poynton* we have seen a single situation expanding into a plot — in M. Gide's novel *Les Faux-Monnayeurs*, we see a plot built out of disparate incidents.

There is first the group of young students and artists who were concerned with a traffic in counterfeit money in 1906 — the mixture of false coin, and literary discussion appeals to the imagination, and the obvious symbolism will leap to the eye of anyone who has ever frequented any sort of literary or artistic circle; for such circles have (figuratively speaking) generally much more false coin than true in circulation.

The second principal theme is taken from the very curious suicide of a boy of fifteen in the class-room of a Lycée at Clermont-Ferraud in 1909. The boy belonged to an association in which his fellow-pupils appear to have mutually urged each other towards suicide.[9]

The two incidents seem to have been linked together in M. Gide's mind by his interest in 'motiveless crimes', and it is significant that at first he intended the chief character of this novel to be Lafcadio. Lafcadio dropped out of *Les Faux-Monnayeurs*: he is the hero of *Les Caves du Vatican*, in which he commits a motiveless murder. His temporary juxtaposition with the story of the counterfeit coin and the suicide story must have helped M. Gide to bring them together: motiveless, or nearly motiveless criminality is the link between them. His students make very little profit out of their false money.

Incidents and characters out of the author's past, which we have met in a more nearly raw state in *Si le Grain ne Meurt*, were adapted, and used to fill in the gaps. Moreover the daily life of an artist engaged upon a serious work may sometimes seem to take on the pattern of that work, and may throw out scraps which can be incorporated in it — such scraps, offerings of life, are recorded together with his own mental work on the novel by M. Gide in that extremely interesting document, the *Journal des Faux-Monnayeurs*.

§ 6 A PLOT UNSUCCESSFULLY DEDUCED FROM ONE EPISODE: 'ADAM BEDE'

Sometimes an author has been fascinated by a single incident, not in itself the whole subject of the novel, and has discovered his subject after following up the clues given in that incident. An example of a not-very-good plot deduced from one striking incident is *Adam Bede*.

The story was suggested to George Eliot by an incident in the life of her aunt, Mrs. Samuel Evans, a Methodist preacher. Mrs. Samuel Evans had once spent a night in prison with a girl convicted of child-murder, had prevailed on her to make a confessoin of her guilt, and had next day attended her to the gallows. G. H. Lewes, with whom George Eliot was living, remarked that the night in prison would make a good scene in a novel — and *Adam Bede* was constructed to lead up to and down from that scene.[10]

This scene started George Eliot off with two indispensable characters — Dinah Morris, the Methodist preacher, and Hetty Sorrel, the seduced village maiden. She had the good idea to make them antecedently connected, to add poignancy to the prison scene, and to make it arise more naturally out of the action. She therefore gave them an uncle and aunt in common, a farmer and his wife, the latter one of the comic, rustic characters in which she excelled.

At the farm, of course, Hetty met her seducer; the plot evidently requires a seducer, and who more fit for the role, by all traditions, than the young officer, heir to the village squire?

To get the full pathos out of the story, the girl is given a true lover of her own class, with honourable intentions: this is Adam Bede. Lewes suggested that the novel ought to end with Adam's marriage to the woman preacher, and this certainly makes a neat, rounded conclusion. He also wished for a clash of some sort between the true lover and the seducer — and while she was listening to *Wilhelm Tell* at the Munich opera, it occurred, we are told, to George Eliot to make the rivals fight. Tell's adventures must have been her inspiration, and it is amusing to follow a great novelist's mind so closely.[11]

George Eliot softened the story given in her data in two respects. Hetty is not really guilty of murder, but only of temporary desertion of her baby; and she is not hanged. At the last minute, thanks to her lover's energy, the sentence is commuted to transportation, and she goes to Botany Bay. Probably it was right to make these changes. Hetty is naturally more sympathetic for not being a murderess, and the book is less melodramatic because she is not hanged — Hardy did not do well to hang Tess. The changes, however, add to the faults of construction.

It is a fatal weakness in *Adam Bede* that the great prison scene, which more than any other scene remains in the memory, the scene round which the book was written, does not advance the plot at all. Hetty's confession does not tell us anything that we did not already know, and has no influence upon her fate. If she had indeed been hanged, it might have given us a melancholy satisfaction to know that she had confessed her crime, and died penitent; but she was only transported. Sir Leslie Stephen well points out how ineffective in fact Dinah Morris is, and how much more Jeanie Deans, with whom her situation may in some ways be compared, contributes to the plot of *The Heart of Midlothian*.

Lewes was quite right in thinking the prison scene would be impressive in a novel — it is. As he was not a novelist it is not surprising if he never thought about the constructional difficulties which such a scene implies. However, it is a peevish sort of criticism that harps upon the imperfections that inevitably go with certain excellences. One cannot see — and George Eliot evidently could not see — how this scene could occur in a perfect novel. Yet it is one of the great scenes in nineteenth-century fiction, and it is much better to have it in an imperfectly constructed book, than not to have it at all.

§ 7 A PLOT SUCCESSFULLY DEDUCED FROM ONE EPISODE: 'THE AMBASSADORS'

Adam Bede, then, is a plot unsuccessfully deduced from one striking incident. To find a plot successfully deduced from one incident, we naturally turn back to Henry James. Unlike *The Spoils of Poynton*, the expansion of a situation, *The Ambassadors* springs from one single incident. The incident is not so dramatic as the night which Mrs. Samuel Evans spent with the infanticide; it is again 'the merest grain, the speck of truth', that Henry James loved.

This is the 'little germ'. A young friend of his, in Whistler's garden in Paris, had spoken with a distinguished American author, also a friend of Henry James's. The older man had vigorously exhorted his young friend to live, not to miss life.

This incident, and its background, were etched into his mind. He began to ask himself: 'What would be the story to which it would most inevitably form the centre?'[12]

'It is part', he goes on to say, 'of the charm attendant on such questions that the "story" . . . puts on from this stage the authenticity of concrete existence. It then *is*, essentially — it begins to be, though it may more or less obscurely lurk; so that the point is not in the least what to make of it, but only, very delightfully and very damnably, where to put one's hand on it.'

Henry James began by putting his hand on the character who should pronounce the exhortation in the Paris garden. He saw him as a man who felt that he had missed life, who was beginning to be dissatisfied with himself, who had come in a frame of mind that was undergoing change, who was in a mental false position. 'The false position for him was obviously to have presented himself at the gate of that boundless menagerie' (that is, Paris) 'primed with a moral scheme of the most approved pattern which was yet framed to break down on any approach to vivid facts; that is to any at all liberal appreciation of them.'

There was one obvious difficulty — in the Anglo-Saxon world, and particularly in Puritan America, Paris is vulgarly associated with the most banal naughtiness, and with the coarsest and most commonplace breakdowns of the moral schemes of Anglo-Saxon visitors. Henry James was very anxious to have no association of this sort about his book, and indeed there is nothing common or mean to be found in *The Ambassadors*. The theme is a serious one — of a missionary sent to convert the inhabitants of a country who, through no mental or moral collapse, but rather through the breakdown of his illiberal, fixed opinions, learns to admire their standpoint more than his own, and is converted to it.

Strether, the chief of the ambassadors, is sent to Europe by an American lady, whom he much admires, to reclaim her son who is staying in Paris, where he is believed to be retained by a woman who has some hold upon him. He is wanted at home to take his part in the family business — the 'manufacture of a small, trivial, rather ridiculous object of the commonest domestic use'. We are never told what this object is, it is left to our guess. However, when Strether gets to Paris he is so charmed by European artistic life that business life in America seems less and less the obviously better way of living that he had first thought it. So far from wanting to reclaim the young man to his status as a good American, and as manufacturer of the 'small, trivial, rather ridiculous object', he wants to turn himself into a good European, and regrets that he is starting so late.

§ 8 THE PLOT AS A PRE-EXISTING PATTERN,
TO WHICH NOVELISTS WORK

After considering Henry James, and the evolution of his plots, it is a shock to remember how haphazardly some authors (and the greatest are among them), have chosen the outline for their books. It will help us here if we borrow Mr. Forster's distinction between the 'plot' and the 'story'.[13] Writers of this sort are generally most interested in character, and their characters turn their stories into plots by the little twists they give to them.

The outline of the story may be lifted from elsewhere; it may even be a stock plot that many have used before. Shakespeare followed this method, so does Jane Austen in her early novels. A young woman goes for the first time into the world, a young man helps her out of an embarrassment, she falls in love with him, and after delays and difficulties they are eventually married. Two sisters are separated by misunderstandings from the men with whom they are in love, until a series of events brings them together again, and all is well. It is the detailed working up of these stories into plots that is fascinating to us, and it is the characters who do that working up. The story remains as a form of discipline, preventing the characters from straggling about aimlessly, narrowing but deepening the channels along which they may develop.

RESULTING FROM GROWTH, NOT MANIPULATION

Some novelists will even look outside literature for a pattern. Mr. Aldous Huxley advises would-be writers to look at the relations between a couple of cats, for instance, and to translate them into human terms. Had he done so, he might indeed have found more interesting plots there than those of his later novels; and he would at least have presented a psychology so far agreeable to Masson as to hold good 'in a world of imaginary cats'.[14]

Some novelists have been inspired by the moves on a chess-board, or by the rules of other games. Meredith in *The Egoist* certainly had in mind (for both in the name of his chief character, Sir Willoughby Patterne, and in incidental symbolism he insists on it) the pairings and separations and reshufflings of couples which take place on a willow-pattern plate.

Other novelists have taken the patterns of some well-known classic for their own pattern; and the perception of this pattern working itself out in their novels is no doubt supposed to add to the reader's pleasure. The use of the Odyssey in this way by Fielding and by Joyce is the most obvious example: the *Oedipus Rex* and the book of Tobit have also been used by contemporary writers — no doubt the list could be added to extensively.

It is hard, however, to regard this kind of applied pattern as more than a curiosity of literature, a monstrosity like those seventeenth-century poems that were written in the shape of an altar or of a pair of wings. And if the work made on this pattern happens to be a work of genius, we tend to ignore the pattern.

§ 9 THE PLOT SHOULD RESULT FROM
GROWTH, NOT MANIPULATION

When the plot of the novel has been conceived, by whatever means, it demands faithfulness from the writer. 'One must do as one has conceived', says Flaubert. The process of working out one's conception in fiction is not at all like arranging flowers, putting this here, that there, and giving a pull or a twist to a leaf or a spray in order to make it stand out. It is very much more like giving birth to a baby. Miss Rebecca West has compared it to the growth of a tree.

'For the non-sentimental artist,' she says, 'has an intention of writing a book on a theme which is as determined and exclusive as the tree's intention of becoming a tree, and by passing all his material through his imagination and there experiencing it, he achieves the same identity with what he makes as the growing tree does. Now neither tree nor artist has eyes, neither has ears, neither is intelligent; simply they are becoming what they make. The writer puts out his force and it becomes a phase of his story, as the tree puts out its force and makes a branch. Both know how much force to put out, and where to reassert it, because having achieved this identification with their creation they would feel a faulty distribution of balance as one would a withered limb . . . But the sentimental artist is becoming nothing . . . He is playing a game, he is moving certain objects according to certain rules in front of spectators . . . He sees that one of these objects occupies a certain position on the ground, and knows that he will score a point if he can move it to another position; he therefore sends another of these objects rolling along to displace it. *Shock* . . . one hears the ugly sound.'[15]

If we look back for a moment we can compare and contrast the methods of George Eliot and Henry James. George Eliot manipulates her people to get action and contrast, and listens to Lewes when he says: 'don't you think, Marian, you could put in this, or that?' Whereas Henry James does not play that sort of game; he sits still, watching for the story that 'more or less obscurely lurks', not in the least worrying about what to make of it, but 'only, very delightfully and damnably' where to put his hand on it.

On an altogether lower level of seriousness are such toyings with the novelist's art of those writers who, in Miss Austen's words, stretch out their books with 'solemn specious nonsense, about something unconnected with the story; an essay on writing, a critique on Walter Scott, or the history of Bonaparte. . . .'

Yet whether the plot results from the expansion of a situation, like *The Spoils of Poynton*, the linking together of incidents, like *Les Faux-Monnayeurs*, or the deductions drawn from one incident, like *Adam Bede* or *The Ambassadors*, the process which goes on in the novelist's mind, all the ways in which he works on his material, are more analogous to discovery than to invention. The story has early put on 'the authenticity of concrete existence'; the author asks himself 'what really happened?' not 'what shall I make happen next, to amuse my readers?'

And here we are up against the impenetrable residuum that is left, no matter how many external aspects of the novelist's creative activity we look at. Mrs. Wharton is right — we cannot put into words 'exactly what happens at that "fine point of the soul" where the creative act, like the mystic's union with the unknowable, really seems to take place'.

§ 10 THE NOVELIST AS MYSTIC: 'THE SONG OF HENRY JAMES'

Here is no place for the discussion of the nature of mysticism. Let us take the definition given by William James. He enumerates four 'marks' of mystical experience: ineffability — it cannot adequately be put into words, it can only be hinted at, or described by analogy; noetic quality — some knowledge is always conveyed; transiency and passivity — it can neither be summoned nor retained at will.[16]

With this in mind — unless we restrict the word 'mystical' to a religious sense — if we turn to Henry James's astonishing colloquy with his genius, we are unable to deny it the title of mystical writing. Though it does not tell us 'exactly what happens', it throws some light on the mystical nature of the creative act.

'I needn't expatiate on this — on the sharp consciousness of this hour of the dimly-dawning New Year, I mean; I simply make an appeal to all the powers and forces and divinities to whom I've ever been loyal and who haven't failed me yet — after all: never, never yet! Infinitely interesting — and yet somehow with a beautiful sharp poignancy in it that makes it strange and rather exquisitely formidable, as with an unspeakable deep agitation, the whole artistic question that comes up for me in the train of this idea . . . of the *donnée* for a situation that I began here the other day to fumble out. I mean I come back, I come back yet again and again, to my only seeing it in the dramatic way — as I can only see everything and anything now . . . Momentary side-winds — things of no real authority — break in every now and then to put their inferior little questions to me; but I come back, I come back, as I say, I all throbbingly and yearningly and passionately, oh mon bon, come back to this way that is clearly the only one in which I can do anything now, and that will open out to me more and more, and that has overwhelming reasons pleading all beautifully in its breast. What really happens is that the closer I get to the problem, to the application of it in any particular case, the more I get *into* the application, so that the more doubts and torments fall away from me, and the more I know where I am, the more everything spreads and shines and draws me on and I'm justified of my logic and my passion . . . Causons, causons, mon bon — oh celestial, soothing, sanctifying process, with all the high sane forces of the sacred time fighting through it, on my side. Let me fumble it gently and patiently out — with fever and fidget laid to rest — as in the old enchanted months. It only looms, it only shines and shimmers, *too* beautiful and too interesting; it only hangs there too rich and too full and with too much to give and to pay; it only presents itself too admirably and too vividly, too straight and square and vivid, as a little organic and effective Action. . . .

Thus just these first little wavings of the oh so tremulously passionate little old wand (now!) make for me, I feel, a sort of

88

NOTES

promise of richness and beauty and variety; a sort of portent of the happy presence of the elements ... I seem to emerge from these recent bad days — the fruit of blind accident — and the prospect clears and flushes, and my poor blest old Genius pats me so admirably and lovingly on the back that I turn, I screw round, and bend my lips to passionately, in my gratitude, kiss its hands.'[17]

NOTES

1. *Partial Portraits* (Essay on Maupassant).
2. *The Art of the Novel: critical prefaces*, ed. Richard P. Blackmur (1935), p. 119. *The Portrait of a Lady*, however, began in 'the sense of a single character', ibid., p.42.
3. ibid.
4. loc. cit., p. 121.
5. loc. cit., p. 221.
6. loc. cit., p. 120.
7. *The Craft of Fiction.*
8. See especially *Du Côté de chez Swann*, I, pp. 229-37, and *La Prisonnière*, II, pp. 79-85. In fact it was the friend who performed the act of atonement to Vinteuil, but she was inspired by his daughter's veneration for him. (Mr. Raymond Mortimer has pointed out to me a more probable origin for the Montjouvian story, cf. *Le Sabbat* by Maurice Sachs (1946) p. 285.)
9. *Journal des Faux-Monnayeurs.*
10. *George Eliot* by Leslie Stephen (English Men of Letters Series), pp. 64-5.
11. ibid., p. 66.
12. loc. cit., p. 311.
13. *Aspects of the Novel, passim.*
14. v, p. 27.
15. *The Strange Necessity* (1928), pp. 16 ff.
16. *Varieties of Religious Experience*, p. 380.
17. *The Letters of Henry James*, ed. Percy Lubbock (1920), vol. I, pp. xx-xxi.

CHAPTER V

THE MAKING OF CHARACTER

§ I CHARACTERS IN SOME WAY, ALWAYS,
TAKEN FROM LIFE

HENRY JAMES, for whom the starting-point in the creation of his novels was generally a fragment of plot, gives an interesting account of the completely opposite method used by his friend Turgenieff. 'The germ of a story, with him, was never an affair of plot — that was the last thing he thought of: it was the representation of certain persons. The first form in which a tale appeared to him was as the figure of an individual, or a collection of individuals, whom he wished to see in action, being sure that such people must do something very special and interesting. They stood before him, definite, vivid, and he wished to know, and to show as much as possible of their nature. The first thing was to make clear to himself what he did know to begin with; and to this end he wrote out a sort of biography of each of his characters, and everything they had done and that had happened to them up to the opening of the story. He had their *dossier*, as the French say, and as the police has that of every conspicuous criminal.'[1]

It was in life that Turgenieff found the first suggestions for his people. He stated that he could not create character at all, unless he fixed his imagination upon a living person: without a definite person in mind he could not give vitality and idiosyncrasy to his creation.[2] It is probable that this practice is almost universal. The note which is frequently placed at the beginning of a novel, and which announces: 'Every character in this book is entirely fictitious' is nearly always a lie. It is difficult to see what it is there for, since it deceives nobody, and would be no protection in a libel action. One must suppose that the common explanation is the true one: it is inserted by publishers so that illiterate booksellers' assistants may more easily be able to distinguish fiction from biography, memoirs and the like.

If a character is 'wholly fictitious', then we can be quite sure it is drawn largely from other characters in fiction, themselves in some way first drawn from life.

This is not to say that the novelist often puts people just as they are into his books, a thing which his acquaintance seem to fear and hope. For life and art are very different things, and existence in one is very different from existence in the other. For one thing, life enforces on us a continuous existence, whereas a character in fiction does not exist except at such times as he appears on the scene. And the fictional character must not appear too often on the scene without doing something very special and interesting — while all of us live days or years without doing anything very special and interesting.

Many of us, very likely, have little or nothing to give to the novelist, who has not the reasons that the Almighty appears to have for creating people who are not interesting. He should accept this difference, and not falsely reason that he *ought* to be able to interest himself in any person God has made. It is necessary for him to free himself from the tyranny of old tags like *quidquid agunt homines* or *homo sum, nihil humani â me alienum* — which seem to have a peculiarly binding force on those who know no other Latin, and which lead to such artistic idiocies as the cult of the 'little man' as hero.

§ 2 ATTEMPTS TO RENDER THE WHOLE MAN IN FICTION: JOYCE, VIRGINIA WOOLF

Mr. Forster has drawn an illuminating distinction between *homo sapiens* and *homo fictus*: among other things, he points out how free *homo fictus* is from work, and what a disproportionate amount of time he devotes to love.

Probably the only serious attempt to make *homo fictus* coextensive with *homo sapiens* is that of James Joyce. Though the characters of other authors are often seen eating, Joyce's Bloom is almost unique in fiction because he also digests his meals. But the experiment fails for three reasons — firstly, Bloom's acts and thoughts are as much a selection from his total twenty-four hours' experience as those of any other fictional character: a book many times longer even than *Ulysses* would be required to contain all a man's acts and thoughts in that space of time. Secondly, the absence of selection is, however, carried so far that much of what Bloom does and thinks is neither special nor interesting. Thirdly, it is impossible to develop any other character in the book on the same scale. You can only have one such close approximation to a *homo sapiens* in a book; the rest must be *homines ficti*. Therefore we have a solipsistic world in which one man is real and the rest fictitious. This is not so convincing a picture of the real world as even those fictions in which none but *homines ficti* appear. There are many of them on the same level of reality, and they can have their approximations to human loves and hates.

Not only does man in fiction commonly omit such external acts as washing his teeth, but his interior or mental life is correspondingly simplified. He proceeds from thought to thought, or from feeling to feeling, either in accordance with reason or with an easily understood process of association of ideas. He will not suddenly burst out singing, nor will he suddenly be overwhelmed by misery — he will be better-controlled than real people often are.

Virginia Woolf's characters, however, show all the passing moods of real people — the moods pass so quickly and are so varied that it is difficult to sum up any one of them in a few words. She has done one thing that Joyce has not, she has evolved a technique for showing more than one character, who is an approximation to *homo sapiens*, in action at the same time — but whereas Bloom is a solid person, with fine vitality and idiosyncrasy, Mrs. Woolf's characters are all alike. The nearest she gets to showing real processes of thought and feeling — in *The Waves* — the most completely identical are her characters.

The book is a sextet of disembodied voices, beautiful and sometimes wise voices, but very hard to tell apart. Though Mrs. Woolf certainly conveys to the world 'the most thorough knowledge of human nature', and conveys it in 'the best chosen language', yet there is next to no 'delineation of its varieties'.

The truth is perhaps this: while we know the characters of Miss Austen as we know our friends (if we are abnormally observant), we know Mrs. Woolf's characters as we know ourselves. We know more and less about ourselves than about anyone else: we are all like the man in the scriptures who beholdeth himself in a glass, and straightway he goeth away and forgetteth what manner of man he is. We know so many changes in our expressions, that we hardly know what our faces are like. We know all our thoughts and actions, and they are so inconsistent that it is hard for any one of us to sum up his character in a few words, or even to be sure that he has a character at all. We are all alike, made of the same elements, but in different proportions: it is hard for us to stand back from ourselves, and to see what the proportions are in our own case — and it is hard to stand back in this way from the characters of Mrs. Woolf.

§3 'FLAT CHARACTERS': DICKENS

The opposite to the character which tries to reproduce the whole man, is what Mr. Forster has called the 'flat character'. He is summed up in a single phrase, such as: 'I will never desert Mr. Micawber', which sums up all Mrs. Micawber's nature and actions. The creation of the flat character is best studied not in fiction, but in drama, in Ben Jonson's theory of 'humours', and the best statement on the subject is that made by his most recent editors in the introduction to their monumental edition.

'He seizes character under one aspect, because he sees it so; neglecting, because he does not see them, the cross-play of impulses, the inconsistencies and conflicts, mingled strength and weakness, of which they are normally composed. His observation was prodigiously active and acute; but its energy was spent in accumulating observations of a single dominant trait, not in distinguishing fine shades. The nuances fell together for him, and the vast complexes of detail which his voracious eye collected, and his unsurpassed memory retained, grouped themselves round a few nuclei of ludicrous character . . . his personages are real men seen from a particular angle, not moral qualities translated into their human embodiments.'[3]

This is an extremely acute analysis of the way in which Jonson's mind must have worked when he was creating character, and it will stand for much of Dickens's character-creation as well. Not for nothing was Dickens an admirer of Jonson, and fond of impersonating his soldier-braggart Bobadil. Many of Dickens's most memorable characters, while 'flat' are yet 'real men seen from a particular angle, not moral qualities translated into their human embodiments'. We even know some of the real men exposed to this angular vision — for instance that Mr. Micawber and Old Dorritt are portraits of Dickens's father, seen from different angles, and Mr. Skimpole is a portrait of Leigh Hunt — they are not just embodiments of different types of fecklessness and irresponsibility.

In drama, where there is little time for subtlety, for more than a few characters to exhibit inconsistencies and conflicts and developments, it would be even harder than in fiction to get on without 'flat' characters. And in fiction their value is inestimable: almost every successful comic character is 'flat'. For when a comic character begins to put on three-dimensionality, to abandon his stock phrase, and to say something else — most of all when he appears tired of entertaining us, and seems to want our sympathy — we are generally displeased. He is apt to become sentimental. And as a corollary, those who in life have chosen to present a 'flat' picture of themselves to the world, a thing which it is often convenient to do, show better taste if they keep it up to the end: 'the clown with the breaking heart' is an abomination.

Leaving on one side the experiments of Joyce and of Virginia Woolf, and on the other the 'flat' character, who is found in his most impressive form in the works of Dickens, the 'round' character of fiction is generally a compromise between Everyman in and Everyman out of his Humour. There are enough stable elements in his character for him to be seen as a character, and yet he still retains the power to surprise us — if he is successful he will surprise us in such a way, that, though his action was unexpected, yet we do not think it improbable — it is rather a revelation to us that he could act in such a way. And the subtler his drawing is, the more it should be possible for readers to disagree about whether he is a good character or no. That is, there should be no doubt that he is well drawn, but there may be very different opinions whether he is virtuous or agreeable. So wicked is the human heart that even the best of men, if fully known, would have much in them to disgust us — and there is no reason to disbelieve the Saints who, in their autobiographical writings, insist on their own depravity.

The successfully drawn character in fiction will certainly be no better than the Saints. Jane Austen, in her mock synopsis of a novel on a theme suggested by the Prince Regent's librarian, came to this climax of delightful absurdity: 'the scene will be for ever shifting from one set of people to another, but there will be no mixture: all the good will be unexceptionable in every respect. There will be no foibles or weaknesses but with the wicked, who will be completely depraved and infamous, hardly a resemblance of humanity left in them.' She might almost have been describing *Eyeless in Gaza*.

The unfortunate thing about the characters in that novel is that they are all quite inhuman. Either they indulge in promiscuous love on a sub-human level, and if any of them in the course of his amours experiences any genuine feeling, he is made to look foolish; or on the other hand they dabble in mysticism, and cease to look for any happiness in earthly things. They are more or less than human, angels or apes.

The answer to Disraeli's question, whether Man is an angel or an ape, is of course that he is neither — he is Man, perhaps a poor thing to be, though some people have made quite a good thing of it. And in Man Mr. Huxley is not much interested. He has written somewhere that Man can, as Man, expect no happiness — there is only happiness on the animal or spiritual level.

This is pernicious nonsense. Though some people are able to live on an entirely spiritual level, it is a matter of vocation — no religion has ever supposed that everyone was called to this plane. Is only animality left for everyone except a chosen few? On the contrary, although there are only too good reasons to suppose that Man can as Man expect no lasting happiness — we have here no abiding city — yet there is an enormous range of happiness that is specifically human, and that would make no appeal to an animal or a pure spirit.

If it is bad ethically to dismiss Man in this way, it is worse aesthetically. On an anti-human philosophy no good fiction can be built. The novel is about human beings. Physiology, Psychology, Biography, Hagiography may deal with the brute or the saint, with Heliogabalus or St. Theresa: they are outside the field of the novelist. Though one would be unwilling so to limit the novelist's range that holiness and brutality are excluded altogether from his picture, it is safe to say that a fictional character who was utterly holy or utterly brutal would not be a success except in a very minor role.

The characters in a novel, then, are neither to be 'unexceptionable' nor 'completely depraved', but a mixture of good and bad, like the characters we know in real life, from self-knowledge or from observation. No doubt each character does best on the whole if he keeps an even tenor, and acts from what one might call the centre of his character. It is not at all the duty of the novelist to show us how much good there is in the worst of us, or how much bad in the best of us.

Nevertheless, he has this power in reserve, and some extremely striking and moving scenes in fiction do depend on the use of the final resources of a character for good or evil. Such a scene as that in *A High Wind in Jamaica*, where a small girl is shown (fairly convincingly) as capable of committing a very cruel murder, may be called a mere *tour de force*. But there are few things more admirable in Proust than the delicate and inspired generosity, the self-sacrifice of Monsieur and Madame Verdurin on behalf of the impoverished Saniette, on the very evening of their atrocious and final act of treacherous cruelty to Monsieur de Charlus.[4] And the novels of Miss Compton-Burnett afford many instances of acts of beautiful and intelligent sympathy performed by terribly tyrannical and possessive people.

§ 5 THE RELATION OF FICTIONAL CHARACTERS TO THEIR 'ORIGINALS'

Yet for all their likeness to real people, fictional characters are not real people: they do not have to function in life, but in the novel, which is an art form. They function in plots, which are abstractions, patterns, conventions — and they themselves are, like the plots they function in, abstractions, patterns, conventions. It is quite common to find critics, and even novelists themselves, dismiss Plot with some impatience, but discuss Character with much more seriousness — and yet they are of the same order of creation.

The fictional character is therefore seldom the portrait of a living person, and more often a pattern or sketch suggested by a living person. It is on this account not surprising that character is often invented on a slender basis of observation, and is not often the result of the prolonged study by a writer of any particular individual. 'The writer', says Somerset Maugham, 'does not copy his originals; he takes what he wants from them, a few traits that have caught his attention, a turn of mind that has fired his imagination, and therefrom constructs his

G   97

character. He is not concerned whether it is a truthful likeness; he is concerned only to create a plausible harmony convenient for his own purposes.'[5]

The biographer's method of research into further details, that he may know all that can be known of his original, and his purpose to draw a truthful likeness, even if the truth be neither plausible nor harmonious, is the exact opposite of the method and purpose of the novelist, who only requires enough knowledge of his original to fire his imagination. Both methods of character-creation are used by us in everyday life, when we are trying to get to know other people, or when we are making conversation about them. In the case of people who really matter to us, we are like biographers — anything about them is interesting and important to us. But more often we find it amusing to give free rein to the imagination, and to fill up gaps in our knowledge by guess-work — perhaps a more innocent pastime than research into other people's private affairs.

It is with such limitations that we can ask the question where novelists have drawn their characters from, and what relation characters bear to their 'originals'. Novelists have fixed their imaginations on particular persons, certainly, but they have seldom reproduced them realistically. 'Of course there must be a beginning to every conception', writes Miss Compton-Burnett, 'but so much change seems to take place in it at once, that almost anything comes to serve the purpose — a face of a stranger, a face in a portrait, almost a face in the fire.'[6] We should not be much advanced in our study of a writer's art if we knew what faces had served his purpose. Letters and Diaries of authors, where they exist, of course can only be regarded as early sketches of the people mentioned in them; the change has begun — and we never see mere raw material that a writer has worked up later. A writer is a writer, even if he is only writing his diary, or a private letter.

Of Emily Brontë, for example, we know that her imagination was fed on country gossip and legend in a country rich in eccentrics, solitary houses, and terrible stories — where it was a traditional saying: 'keep a stone in thy pocket seven years; turn it, and keep it seven years longer, that it may be ever ready to thine hand when thine enemy draws near.' And her sister Charlotte wrote of her: 'I am bound to avow that she had scarcely more practical knowledge of the peasantry amongst whom she lived, than a nun has of the country-people that pass her convent gates . . . intercourse with them she never sought, nor, with a few exceptions, ever experienced; and yet she knew them, knew their ways, their language, their family histories; she could hear of them with interest, and talk of them with detail, minute, graphic and accurate; but with them she rarely exchanged a word.'[7] This is all we know, or need to know, of the genesis of Heathcliff — a 'germ', picked up in this way, developed on solitary moorland walks, or in the fire-light of a home where life was both dramatic and intellectual.

Other novelists have begun from a face seen in the street or in a train, from a chance word overheard. It is enough to have seen or heard something significant, and the novelist is haunted — and 'haunted' is the right word for it — until the character has been given life. The process of character-procreation is like that in the procreation-myth in Samuel Butler's *Erewhon*; the unborn are determined to be born, and haunt and plague their future parents, and give them no rest until they haue brought them into the world. And like the 'story' for Henry James, at an early stage embryonic characters put on 'the authenticity of concrete existence'.

It will depend on the mind of the writer whether the first hint of a character is more often audible or visible.

Oscar Wilde found two characters and a famous short story in the Louvre. He told the story to the two ladies who composed the single personality of the poet, 'Michael Field'. He had been fascinated by the Infanta of Velasquez, with the rose in her hand. 'He was bent', says Michael Field, 'on learning the history of that rose, and found it in a portrait near at hand of a dwarf. Now the princess — let history go off with her rags

— had given the dwarf that rose — the dwarf was dancing before the court, and she took it from her hair and flung it to him. He went away in rapture at the consciousness of her love . . . then the doctrine of doubles, and inattention on my part — ultimately the dwarf discovers from a mirror his own hideousness, and when they come in and try to raise him to dance, lies stretched responseless. He is dead — dead, they tell the princess, of a broken heart. She replies going away — "Let those who love me have no hearts" . . . "Fiction, not truth — I could never have any dealings with truth — if truth were to come unto me, to my room, he would say to me, 'you are too wilful'. And I should say to him, 'you are too obvious'. And I should throw him out of the window." Michael: "you would say to *him*. Is not truth a woman?" "Then I could not throw her out of the window; I should bow her to the door." [8]

Jane Austen, on the other hand, went round picture galleries, after the completion of *Pride and Prejudice*, hoping to find portraits of Elizabeth and Jane. We must not take this little joke of hers, in a family letter, too seriously; but it does suggest that she had not completely visualized them, but would have known them if she saw them.

Since characters are generally built up on a slender basis, it is a common experience for an author to be accused of having drawn a malicious portrait of a living person in some character for which that person has provided no suggestion. And in cases where the same person has provided suggestions for more than one fictional character, those characters may very well bear little or no resemblance to each other. Compare the pedant, Casaubon in *Middlemarch* with the miser, Professor Forth in *Belinda*: George Eliot and Rhoda Broughton drew these two very dissimilar characters, as we know, from Mark Pattison — and there are plenty of materials for a biography of Mark Pattison, with which they could be contrasted. Compare the mean-spirited young man drawn by Lawrence from Peter Warlock in *Women in Love*, with the Rabelaisian figure whom Aldous Huxley drew from the same original in *Antic Hay*.

Or compare Dickens's two portraits of his own father, as Mr. Micawber or as Old Dorritt. They are not much alike; nor are Flora Finching and Dora Copperfield, who had the same original.

§6 AUTOBIOGRAPHICAL FICTION

There are of course novels, and great novels, that are almost purely autobiographical, and in these, as in some other novels there are characters drawn from assignable persons, and intended as portraits. We know from what personal experience parts of *Les Faux-Monnayeurs*, and almost all *The Way of All Flesh* derive. Butler says that writing his novel was 'a kind of picking up of sovereigns', for 'the novel contains records of things I saw happening, rather than imaginary incidents'.[9] M. Gide makes Edouard, his novelist within the novel, say: 'I always have the greatest difficulty in "making-up" the truth. Even to change the colour of the hair seems to me a fraud, which for me makes the truth less lifelike.'[10]

But even in such novels the character has to be shown in scenes, which must be invented and manipulated by an art entirely different from the biographer's. The author must pass his material through his imagination, and there re-experience it — he must become one with his characters in a way in which he was not one with them in real life. And since people in life, as Miss Compton-Burnett says, 'hardly seem to be definite enough to appear in print',[11] their definition has to be increased. To take a metaphor from the kitchen, they must be 'reduced', as soup is 'reduced' to a sufficient strength by boiling away superfluous water. This 'reduction' of a character is one of the processes it goes through in the imagination: observably some characters in fiction have not been sufficiently 'reduced'.

A novelist would not (or should not) feel that he had done less creative work in thus recreating a person whom he had known in real life, than in drawing a character from 'a face in the fire'.

§7 'CONFLATION'

Characters so directly drawn from life are probably rare, at least among novels that are important works of art. It is rare for fictional characters to have their origin each in only one real person. Conflation is probably the most common mode of character-creation, whether the character is round or flat. It is unlikely that, after the event, an author could give a list of all to whom he owed small suggestions for his characters, even if he kept such careful journals as the Goncourts or M. Gide, or even if he were as fanatically interested in his own work as Proust. Curiosity has seized on the characters of Proust with the enthusiasm of scholars seeking to identify an historical site, and there are (or recently were) people alive who claim to 'be' Albertine, Jupien, etc. But of the 'keys' to his novel Proust himself wrote to Lucien Daudet: 'there are so many to each door, that in fact there is none.'[12] And in his novel he wrote: 'there is no name of a fictitious character under which the writer could not put sixty names of people seen: one has posed for the grimace, another for the eyeglass, another for the anger, another for the becoming movement of the arm etc.'[13] Again: 'a book is a vast cemetery, and on most of the graves one can no longer read the obliterated names.'[14]

It is the act of conflation that is *par excellence* the creative act of the novelist: something new arises out of the conflated bits. If the word 'creator' is ever applicable to anyone but God, it may here be used. An analogy may be found in other creative acts of the intelligence, in Inference, or even better, in the making of Metaphors, which Aristotle saw as the act of creative genius: 'for to make good metaphors implies an eye for resemblance.'[15] This 'eye for resemblance' is as important in the creation of character as we saw the 'eye for a subject' to be important in the creation of plot.

The great source of character-creation is of course the novelist's own self. Some form of self-projection must always take place, of reincarnation in the fictional character. The writer, living for the time in his characters, divests himself of those parts of his own nature which are irrelevant, and develops the relevant parts of his nature to more than their normal size — his more successful characters are portraits of potential selves.

This is not to say that he often indulges in self-portraiture: it would not be a good thing to produce in a novel the startling effect which Corvo produced in a painting of the translation of St. William of Norwich, in which more than forty faces were given identical features — his own.

The novelist may have mentally to change his age, sex, social position, and other accidents, and also to develop to the full every suggestion of every vice or virtue he may possess. Here again the creation of character seems not unlike the process whereby we understand other people — since our knowledge of other people is derived from our knowledge of ourselves. 'The material for any picture of personal states', says Henry James, 'will have been drawn preponderantly from the depths of the designer's own mind.'[16] *Know thyself*, is the novelist's first maxim: and the novelist with the widest range as a creator of character is he who contains within himself the greatest variety of potential selves.

There is a perpetual strain between the mould of the character and the novelist's mind that is poured into it — the novelist's mind is always trying to distort the mould, and to make the character more like the author. If writers speak of impersonality in their work, we must not take them quite literally — they mean that they respect the mould. For instance, they will have tried indeed to give a jealous character something of the jealousy which they know in their own hearts, but purified from the idiosyncrasies which it may there have acquired — it has to be not *their* jealousy, but the jealousy of the character.

'I have always forbidden myself to put anything of myself into my work', wrote Flaubert, 'and yet I have put in a great deal . . . I have written most tender pages without love, and boiling pages with no fire in my veins. I have imagined, remembered, combined.'[17]

However, he complained: 'It is difficult to express well what one has never felt.'[18] And again he wrote, of *Madame Bovary*: 'The reason I go so slowly is that nothing in this book is drawn from myself, never can my personality be less useful to me . . . Imagine, I must all the time enter into skins that are anti-pathetic to me. For six months I have been making platonic love, and at the moment I am going into Catholic ecstasies at the sound of church bells, and I want to go to confession.'[19] And yet it was indeed Flaubert himself who was entering into these skins, so antipathetic to him, so much so that he could exclaim: 'I am Madame Bovary!' — so much so that he suffered the physical symptoms of arsenical poisoning, when he was writing about her suicide.[20]

'One must', he said, 'by a mental effort transport oneself into the characters, and not draw them towards oneself.'[21] And he advised a friend, also a writer, to attempt this kind of impersonality: 'you will see how well your characters talk, the moment you stop talking through their mouths.'[22]

It will no doubt depend on the make-up of the author whether, like Flaubert, he loses his own personality in one of the characters he has set in action, or whether, like M. Gide, he has rather the sensation of sitting and listening and looking on, while his characters act and talk.[23] Probably most authors experience a confused mixture of the two experiences, as in our dreams we commonly are at the same time both actors in, and external witnesses of an action.

Even the most unexceptionable writer can, in imagination, enter the skins of very bad characters. Those holy women, 'Michael Field', were seriously troubled in conscience about this necessity, and consulted a priest as to the duties of a Christian dramatic poet who 'must needs deal with sinners and become, as Matthew Arnold says, "what we sing".' Fortunately they consulted a priest as imaginative as he was saintly, who put before them the Incarnation of Christ as an example, and told them that it was the poet's duty to bear sin.[24] And at the other end of the scale there are writers whose lives are infinitely less noble than their work.

But though a writer can make characters very much better or worse than himself, in one way his own nature definitely limits his range: he cannot make them much more witty and intelligent than he is. He can make them more nimble-witted, certainly; he can also endow them with memories much better than his own. They can indulge in long, abstruse and apposite quotations — even in prose. They say things impromptu which he has carefully worked out for them — brilliant writers of dialogue are not always brilliant conversationalists — Dryden was not, for all the sparkling wit of his comedies and satires. Writers often do not use the spoken word very well — a defect which may have helped to make them writers. But a character can only say what his creator puts into his mouth to say. It is very unbecoming, therefore, for a writer to laugh too loudly at the wit of one of his characters, for he is laughing at his own jokes, and he must not applaud their cleverness, which is his own cleverness. Probably no worse example of this sort of bad taste is to be found than the passage in *Evelyn Innes*, where George Moore comments on the very commonplace reflections of one of his characters: 'never had he thought more brilliantly.' Seldom can an author have made a worse gaffe. Much more commendable is M. Gide's sarcasm about two of his people in *Les Faux-Monnayeurs*: 'as their conversation continued to be very witty, there is no need for me to report it here.'

§9 THE 'RIGHTS' OF CHARACTERS

Since we call the making of characters Creation, and since it is in many ways analogous to the way in which human beings are themselves made out of bits and pieces of their ancestors, the novelist, who has breathed life into them, stands towards them in the position of God. They might sing to him in the hundredth psalm:

> Without our aid he did us make,
> We are his flock, he doth us feed,
> And for his sheep he doth us take.

Moreover, himself unmoved, he stands in the midst of them, like the Goddess of Love (whom otherwise he little resembles), rousing their passions and murmuring:

Cras amet qui nunquam amavit, quique amavit cras amet.

A God has a debt to his creatures: Providence. By analogy, it seems that the novelist owes his characters something.

It would be perverse or whimsical to maintain that fictional characters had duties or rights; yet it is hard to find other words for the conviction that a novelist has certain obligations towards them. Perhaps as they are *simulacra* of human beings, we are shocked if they are not treated as we ought to treat other human beings, as ends in themselves, and not as means to ends of our own.

Certainly we ought not to tell lies about them for the sake of the story, as Thackeray tells a lie about Becky — she could not and would not have murdered Josh, and we feel that he is merely trying to blacken her character by this calumny. And he tells a lie about Major Pendennis in order to advance his plot — certainly he was too honourable to have indulged in blackmail. He was a worldly old gentleman, but incapable of real wickedness — incapable, for instance, of the obstinate resentfulness of Colonel Newcome. If characters ever come to a judgment, it may very well be more tolerable in that day for Arthur's uncle than for Clive's father.

Wanton cruelty on the part of an author towards his characters is also shocking. This does not mean that fictional characters need always have things their own way, nor that fiction
should conform to Miss Prism's definition, and end well for
the good and ill for the bad. But the unhappy ending, when it
comes, must be justifiable and necessary. We do not object
to dreadful things happening to Hardy's characters, we know
that it is a law of their being that everything must go wrong
with them — they live in a world of disastrous coincidences, and
are as sure to come to a bad end as the people in *The Beggar's
Opera* are to be hanged or transported. But if the calamities
which sometimes threaten Miss Austen's characters really took
place — if Marianne Dashwood had died of her putrid fever at
Cleveland; if Mr. Bennet had fought a duel with Wickham,
and had been killed; if Louisa Musgrove had never recovered
consciousness after her fall on the Cobb — we should be indignant, and rightly. Yet all these things would be perfectly
possible, and indeed far more probable than almost anything
that happens in *The Return of the Native* or in *Tess of the
d'Urbervilles*.

Stevenson, in a letter to Barrie, makes as good a comment as
one could wish on this point, and cites the classic instance of an
author's cruelty to his people.

'If you are going to make a book end badly, it must end
badly from the beginning. You let yourself fall in love with,
and fondle, and smile at your puppets. Once you had done
that, your honour was committed — at the cost of truth to life
you were bound to save them. It is the blot on *Richard Feverel*,
for instance, that it begins to end well, and then tricks you and
ends ill. But in that case there is worse behind, for the ill-
ending does not inherently issue from the plot — the story had,
in fact, *ended well* after the great last interview between Richard
and Lucy — and the blind, illogical bullet which smashes all
has no more to do between the boards than a fly has to do with
the room into whose open windows it comes buzzing.'

A contemporary instance is possibly worth taking because of

the high reputation that the novel in question enjoys. It may be that herein lies the reason for the great dissatisfaction that some readers feel with it. In *The Death of the Heart* Miss Elizabeth Bowen draws a painful picture of a small girl, cruelly betrayed by her elders, who read her private diary, lay bare her secrets, and play with her affections — we are filled with pity at her heart-rending situation. 'Ah, the exposure indeed, the helpless plasticity of childhood that isn't dear or sacred to *some*body!' wrote Henry James — but his helpless young people, Morgan Moreen, Maisie, Miles and Flora are always dear and sacred to at least one person — to Henry James. Portia Quayne may be dear, but she is not sacred to Miss Bowen who, one cannot help feeling, has betrayed her more cruelly than anyone else — who invites us, as one of her treacherous elders might have done, to look over her shoulder and smile at the child's pathetic diary. Her honour was committed to respect Portia's secrets.

An author, then, must deal honourably with his characters. But for all that we must never forget that characters, if *simulacra* of human beings, are not human beings. We should not, one hopes, had we been living at the time, have been among those who wrote to Richardson, begging him to spare Clarissa's virtue, or among those who wrote to Dickens begging him to spare the life of little Paul Dombey, or little Nell. We are sorry that he abandoned his original, unhappy ending to *Great Expectations*.

A final illustration may help to establish the status of characters in fiction. Monsignor Ronald Knox has written an entertaining sequel to Trollope's Barsetshire novels: in it he has made a number of Barsetshire people embrace Catholicism. Had he been a mission priest in Barchester in real life, this might well have been a part of his duty. But Barsetshire people exist only in fiction, and aesthetically it is far more suitable that they should remain in the Church of England — as Monsignor Knox would probably agree. We have Cardinal Newman's word for the fact that Birmingham people have souls — some of

NOTES

us might have been tempted to doubt this without his authority: 'one has not great hopes from Birmingham', said Mrs.
Elton in *Emma*. But Barchester people, though possibly more
attractive, have no souls to save — that is the difference
between them.

NOTES

1. *Partial Portraits* (1888), p. 314. Turgenieff, unfortunately, is so
   attached to his dossiers that he frequently prints them in full.
2. Somerset Maugham: *The Summing Up*, § 57.
3. Herford and Simpson: *Introduction to Every Man in his Humour*.
4. *La Prisonnière*, II, pp. 163 ff.
5. loc. cit.
6. loc. cit., p. 25.
7. Mrs. Gaskell: *Life of Charlotte Brontë*.
8. *Works and Days from the Journal of Michael Field*, ed. by T. and
   D. C. Sturge Moore (1933), pp. 135-6.
9. *Notebooks*, s.v. 'The Choice of Subjects'.
10. *Les Faux-Monnayeurs*, I, xi.
11. loc. cit., p. 25. And see Appendix I, p. 135 — a most important
    passage by Henry James.
12. cit. Léon Guichard: *Sept études sur Marcel Proust* (Le Caire, 1942);
    p. 95.
13. *Le Temps Retrouvé*, II, pp. 54-5.
14. ibid., p. 59.
15. *Poetics*, xxii. 9.
16. *The Art of the Novel*, p. 221.
17. Flaubert: *Correspondance*, I, p.128. The genesis of Emma Bovary
    is brilliantly studied by Mr. Francis Steegmuller in *Flaubert and
    Madame Bovary* (1947).
18. Flaubert: *Correspondance*, II, p. 149.
19. ibid., II, pp. 198-9.
20. ibid., III, p. 349.
21. ibid., III, p. 331.
22. ibid., III, p. 157.
23. *Journal des Faux-Monnayeurs, passim*.
24. loc. cit., p. 313.

CHAPTER VI

BACKGROUND

§1 DESCRIPTIVE WRITING IS GENERALLY TOO MUCH ESTEEMED

THE aesthetics of descriptive writing have not yet received sufficient attention — it is commonly held in too great esteem, particularly when it occurs in works of fiction. Painting or music that has a strong literary element is now severely criticized. It is time for an attack to be made upon the pictorial element in literature. Mr. Richards, in *Practical Criticism*, has done much to teach us not to look for 'pictures' in Poetry — nevertheless, the Novel is still in need of a purge.

Like many errors in the criticism of fiction, a love of 'descriptions' comes from not taking fiction seriously enough as an art, from not valuing highly enough work in which 'the most thorough knowledge of human nature, the happiest delineation of its varieties, the liveliest effusions of wit and humour are conveyed to the world in the best chosen language'. 'It is only a novel', Miss Austen reproaches young ladies for saying, when they are asked what they are reading — and though Stendhal, Balzac, Flaubert, Dickens, Henry James and Conrad, Tolstoy and Dostoievsky, not to speak of Miss Austen herself, have written since then, a young woman in a novel by Miss Elizabeth Bowen is still ashamed of reading a novel before luncheon: one cannot doubt this shame is true to life.

If the delineation of character in action is not considered serious, the critic will easily be brought to take the delineation of Nature seriously. Since the time of Dr. Arnold there has been a premium on Nature-study in English education, while a 'thorough knowledge of human nature' has, on the contrary, been rather discouraged — understandably, for it is obviously a more desirable hobby for a boy, from a schoolmaster's point of view, to study the habits of sticklebacks or water-voles, rather than those of the Senior Common-room.

Another cause for the prejudices of critics in favour of descriptive writing lies in the vicious distinction between 'style' and 'subject-matter' in which so many of us have been educated. In a descriptive passage in which a novelist is not getting on with his story, it is thought his 'style' has freer play, and can better be displayed — unhappily many novelists have thought this too. False criticism of this sort has exalted Conrad as a painter of sunsets and tropical landscapes, and has obscured his dramatic powers; this great novelist has so often been praised for anything but those qualities which make him great as a novelist, that his reputation has suffered, and his better work has been neglected, particularly by those who might get the most intense pleasure from it.

§ 2 ITS SUBORDINATE PLACE IN THE
NOVEL

Fiction is the delineation of character in action, and the landscape in the background is merely incidental. In travel-books the situation is generally reversed, and it is the landscape that predominates in importance. There is no reason why 'landscape-writing' (if admitted to be a valid form of writing) should not have figures in the foreground, and why these figures should not be fictitious characters, if the author wishes. But such fictionized or moralized travel or guide-books will depend for their chief interest on qualities that have nothing to do with the art of the novelist; and it is in their own interests that we shall refuse to consider such books as *The Plumed Serpent* or the so-called 'novels' of Mr. Prokosch as novels. They are landscapes with figures, and require to be judged by standards of their own, with which we are not at all here concerned.

In fiction that is a representation of characters in action, the background will probably serve a negative rather than a positive purpose. It will be there less for the sake of being what it is, for example, an English country village, as for the sake of not being anywhere else. Its function is limitative, to keep the characters still, and to allow us to concentrate upon them, and upon the happenings. When we can see the characters and the action clearly, then the background may fade out of focus. Similarly St. Ignatius bids us make a 'composition of place' at the beginning of each of the spiritual exercises — to place ourselves, for example, in Hell or Purgatory, or in the place where some scene in the Scriptures was enacted — but the place is presently allowed to fade out of our meditations. A writer returning to his manuscript will often have to make a 'composition of place', also when he shifts his scene; the reader need not so often perform this exercise.

By background is intended primarily that which in a theatre we see on the stage: the sea-coast of Illyria, the palace of Theseus at Troezen, or the like. It is sometimes alleged that fiction, since it does not dispose of the visual effects of drama, ought in some way to supply their place by description. To this argument the best reply is that in the best days of drama there was a good deal of austerity about visual effects: the Greek stage does not appear to have made much difference between the primeval rocks of the *Prometheus Vinctus* and the palace at Troezen of the *Hippolytus*; nor did the Elizabethan stage make much difference between 'a street in London', and the coast of Illyria or the forest of Arden. And it is more imaginatively effective to present drama with simple means than with the distracting pomp of the Edwardian theatre.

Too many stage-directions are boring and confusing if we read a play; if we see them carried out on the stage, the result is a fussy and undignified ritualism. They are worst of all in a novel.

One would hesitate to recommend to a novelist the classic rule of the Théâtre Français that no chair is to appear on the scene unless someone is presently going to sit on it. Interpreted in its full simplicity, this rule has two inconvenient consequences. Firstly, the scene is unnaturally stark and bare — it is common to have in a room more chairs than are in use. Secondly, every chair would thus receive an undue significance — we should look at it, and wonder who was going to sit on it, just as we look at the revolver on the table, and wonder nervously when it is going to go off. It would be a safer rule to keep as near this starkness as we can, without making it too remarkable. This approximates to Miss Austen's practice.

'You describe a sweet place', she wrote to Anna Lefroy, 'but your descriptions are often more minute than will be liked. You give too many particulars of right hand and left.' She herself had parodied this sort of detailed description in *Love and Freindship*: 'A grove of full-grown Elms sheltered us from the East — . A Bed of full-grown Nettles from the West — . Before us ran the murmuring brook and behind us ran the turnpike road. We were in the mood for contemplation and in a Disposition to enjoy so beautiful a spot.'

In reaction from the ancient and gothic of the horror novels, Miss Austen's houses were generally neat, modern edifices, with not much to be said about them. Northanger and Pemberley are to some extent characterized, because they have a function in the plot. Northanger's gothic temptations are too much for Catherine's good sense; and Pemberley makes Mr. Darcy more valued, not for the great possessions, which we always knew he had, but because it stands for cultured and elegant wealth, and for conscientious stewardship of property. The description of Sotherton, on the other hand, was meant to be boring.

Mrs. Rushworth began her relation: 'This chapel was fitted

H   113

up as you see it, in James the Second's time. Before that period, as I understand, the pews were only wainscot; and there is reason to think that the linings and cushions of the pulpit and family-seat were only purple cloth; but this is not quite certain . . .' This scrupulous and boring accuracy about points of no importance is intended to show Jane Austen's contempt for detailed description, as well as the dullness of the Rushworth family.

A very fine example of her simple, low-toned, descriptive writing, intended to throw the human drama into relief, is the scene of Harriet and the Gipsies in *Emma*.

'Miss Smith and Miss Bickerton, another parlour boarder at Mrs. Goddard's, who had been also at the ball, had walked out together, and taken a road, the Richmond road, which, though apparently public enough for safety, had led them into alarm. About half a mile beyond Highbury, making a sudden turn, and deeply shaded by elms on each side, it became for a considerable stretch very retired; and when the young ladies had advanced some way into it, they had suddenly perceived at a small distance before them, on a broader patch of greensward by the side, a party of gipsies. A child on the watch, came towards them to beg; and Miss Bickerton, excessively frightened, gave a great scream, and calling on Harriet to follow her, ran up a steep bank, cleared a slight hedge at the top, and made the best of her way by a short cut back to Highbury. But poor Harriet could not follow. She had suffered very much from cramp after dancing, and her first attempt to mount the bank brought on such a return of it as made her absolutely powerless.'

There could be no quieter description of natural scenery. We are shown, however, precisely what is necessary to the drama of the young ladies' fright — the distance of the spot from the village, the turn of the road which put it out of view, and the shady and therefore sinister stretch of the road in front. The broader patch of greensward was there to accommodate the gipsies — one may think they had pitched their camp on it.

The bank was steep enough to separate Harriet from her more active companion — and, as it was the Richmond road, presently Mr. Frank Churchill came along and rescued her.

Mr. Herbert Read complains that Miss Austen's descriptive prose is not written 'in any mood of compulsion', he complains of 'the lack of internal necessity', and damns her style with the word 'quaintness'.[1] But we ought rather to recollect the purely functional nature of her descriptions, in which we may not properly look for any 'necessity' but that to provide the barely necessary background and props for the action.

Miss Austen is like an early Italian artist, providing an exquisite, neat, clear, little background to her scenes of human action — the background itself untouched by emotion. Other novelists will make more of the background, developing its symbolism in relation to the characters, or even developing it as an end in itself, so that they become the landscape painters of fiction. Others will develop it photographically, with the enormous fidelity to detail of an English nineteenth-century painter.

§ 4 BACKGROUND IN DICKENS: SYMBOLIC

Of the symbolists, Dickens is supreme: he provides vast, Wagnerian settings for his dramas. The Thames in *Our Mutual Friend*, the marshes in *Great Expectations* are symbolic and exciting. They prepare us to see extraordinary things and people — and Dickens's people are big enough to set against their background, while Hardy's are apt to get lost on Egdon Heath. Dickens does not forget that it is for the sake of the human drama that the background is provided. If, in *Bleak House*, it rains in Lincolnshire, it is because it rains in the heart of Lady Dedlock.

'The Waters are out in Lincolnshire. An arch of the bridge in the park has been sapped and sopped away. The adjacent low-lying ground, for half a mile in breadth, is a stagnant river, with melancholy trees for islands in it, and a surface punctured all over, all day long, with falling rain ... The weather, for many a day and night, has been so wet that the trees seem wet through, and the soft loppings and prunings of the workman's axe can make no crash or crackle as they fall. The deer, looking soaked, leave quagmires, where they pass. The shot of a rifle loses its sharpness in the moist air, and its smoke moves in a tardy little cloud towards the green rise, coppice-topped, that makes a background for the falling rain.'

The feeling of damp chill is the physical counterpart to Lady Dedlock's fears, and the remorseless rain a fit background to her approaching ruin. Unfortunately the actual drama in this case, as so often in Dickens, is strained and impossible. A truer pity and terror at Lady Dedlock's plight is produced by the echoing terrace at Chesnay Wold and the Lincolnshire floods, than by the preposterous schemes of Mr. Tulkinghorn. Dickens is a great artist, nevertheless it must be said that it is more creditable to cause pity and terror by the happenings in a story, rather than by the atmosphere.

§5 BACKGROUND IN HARDY

Hardy is more difficult to comment on. In one thing he is superb, in giving to his characters that immediate background, which one can better describe by a change of metaphor, saying that he digs them up by the roots, with the earth on them. No writer is better than he at showing people at their jobs. His countrymen are real countrymen, and we feel the same satisfaction at watching their work, and the same respect for them when they do it as it should be done, that intelligent people generally feel when they see a craft worthily exercised.

Giles Winterborne, in *The Woodlanders*, planting trees with Marty South, is particularly satisfying.

'He had a marvellous power of making trees grow. Although he would seem to shovel in the earth quite carelessly there was a sort of sympathy between himself and the fir, oak or beech that he was operating on; so that the roots took hold of the soil in a few days. When, on the other hand, any of the journeymen planted, although they seemed to go through an identically similar process, one quarter of the trees would die away during the ensuing August.

Hence Winterborne found delight in the work . . . Marty, who turned her hand to anything, was usually the one who performed the part of keeping the trees in a perpendicular position whilst he threw in the mould. . . .

The holes were already dug, and they set to work. Winterborne's fingers were endowed with a gentle conjurer's touch in spreading the roots of each little tree, resulting in a sort of caress under which the delicate fibres all laid themselves out in their proper direction for growth. He put most of these roots towards the south-west; for, he said, in forty years' time, when some great gale is blowing from that quarter, the trees will require the strongest holdfast on that side to stand against it and not fall.

"How they sigh directly we put 'em upright, though while they are lying down they don't sigh at all," said Marty. . . .

She erected one of the young pines into its hold, and held up her finger; the soft musical breathing instantly set in, which was not to cease night or day till the grown tree should be felled — probably long after the two planters should be felled themselves.'

We respect Giles, we respect Gabriel Oak in *Far From the Madding Crowd* for his presence of mind and skill in saving sheep that are blown up with wind after getting in the clover, and in saving hayricks from fire and from a storm. We rather despise people in Hardy's novels who do not really belong to country life, and are not efficient at it — Troy, the soldier, who endangers the hay-harvest by his stupid arrogance, and Jude, the scholar, who cannot kill a pig properly — just as in real life we are apt to despise people who forget to shut gates, or who are afraid of cows or dogs.

Hardy's great excellence in depicting a natural background lies in the fact that he really knows what he is writing about, and that he offers no artificially pretty view of nature — nature is more likely to impress his characters by her unkindness, than in any other way. But he has the defects of these qualities; his close observation of nature may tempt him to a pre-raphaelite accuracy in depicting her, and when he chooses some of her more uncomfortable features to depict like this, the result may be unintentionally comic. For example, there are the various country messes with which Tess covered herself.

'The outskirt of the garden in which Tess found herself had been left uncultivated for some years, and was now damp and rank with juicy grass which sent up mists of pollen at a touch; and with tall blooming weeds emitting offensive smells — weeds whose red and yellow and purple hues formed a polychrome as dazzling as that of cultivated flowers. She went stealthily as a cat through this profusion of growth, gathering cuckoo-spittle on her skirts, cracking snails that were underfoot, staining her hands with thistle-milk and slug-slime, and rubbing off upon her naked arms sticky blights which, though snow-white on the apple-tree trunks, made madder stains on her skin; thus she drew quite near to Clare, still unobserved of him.'

Such a chapter of accidents, such a series of booby tricks played upon Tess by Nature, well enough parallel the booby tricks which Destiny plays on her, as on so many of Hardy's characters. But he never saw that such an accumulation of disasters was farcical, not tragic — part of the technique of the comic pantomime, rather than of the serious novel.

When Nature does not intervene to make Hardy's characters uncomfortable, they are often rather indifferent to her. Egdon Heath is there, vast and brooding, but never of the importance to Eustacia that the Yorkshire moors are to Catherine Earnshaw. Eustacia is urban in her tastes; she would like to go to Paris, or even to Budmouth, which has at least an Esplanade. Neither she nor Wildeve are real creatures of the moors, which look on at their love-making, and dwarf it into philandering.

Though we may begin a story, like Turgenieff, with a group of people, and decide that such people are sure to do something special or interesting, or we may begin, like Henry James, with a happening, and decide that the people who were agents or patients in that happening must have been worth looking at, one way in which we cannot begin is to take an impressive, natural scene, and decide that the people and happenings there must be worth telling about. For people are not so very much influenced by natural beauties, particularly by those that they live amongst — there is no reason at all why the inhabitants of a striking place should in themselves be interesting, or do interesting things. Too grand a scene in the background may overpower the people in the foreground, so that the author will lose more than he gains by his scenic effects. Highbury is really a more satisfactory background for a work of fiction than Egdon, apart from the fact that the people of Highbury are of incomparably greater interest.

§6 CHARACTERS AND BACKGROUND: BALZAC AND FLAUBERT

Hardy has been much praised for his rendering of the sounds on Egdon, in a way possible only to a countryman born and bred. 'Who else', asks Lord David Cecil, 'would realize that the wind made a different noise when it was blowing through hollow or heather or over bare stones, let alone be able to distinguish them?'[2] Yet though Eustacia no doubt heard these noises, and may subconsciously have distinguished them, she was not listening to them, and they do not contribute to her tragedy.

Such irrelevance, and lack of fusion, is common to novelists who excel at and are therefore tempted to overdo natural description. 'All around were the famous hills,' says a good contemporary writer . . . 'magnificent, chameleon hills, shaped like molars and eye-teeth — but in the mist they might as well not be there.' As they were invisible, they might as well not be mentioned — nor, if they had been visible should they have been mentioned unless they had in some way mattered to t e people who were present.

Characters are often too much the prey of violent emotions to pay much attention to their surroundings. It is when he begins to take his eye off his characters that the novelist is most apt, in idleness, to focus it upon their background; it is easy and restful for him. Novelists, says Montherlant, have always made phrases about the setting in which their lovers meet, but it is only the novelists who see the details of this setting. The lovers see nothing, '*engloutis qu'ils sont dans la bouillie pour les chats*'.[3] The reader, who likes concentrating on the people and the happenings, is not refreshed, but annoyed, to have to focus on the herbaceous border in the background.

Yet in some circumstances the background may be so lit up by an emotion as to become particularly significant in a moment of stress. There is a very fine example of this in *Eugénie Grandet*, when Eugénie's young cousin learns of his father's ruin and suicide.

'In the great moments of life, our soul strongly attaches itself to the places where joy or grief rushes upon us. So Charles examined with special attention the box-hedges of this little garden, the pale leaves that were falling, the crumbling of the walls, the irregularity of the fruit-trees, picturesque details that were to remain engraved on his memory, for ever mixed with this supreme hour by a mnemotechnic peculiar to the passions.'

In the same way lightning is said to imprint on a man's body the picture of the tree under which he has been struck.

Parallels can be found in Hardy's poetry, for example in the poem *Neutral Tones*, of which Mr. Middleton Murry writes: 'he declares that he concentrates a whole world of bitterness in a simple vision: the feeling of bitterness of love shapes into its symbol: *Your face, and the God-curst sun, and a tree, and a pond edged with grayish leaves.* A mental process of this kind is familiar to most people. At an emotional crisis in their lives some part of their material surroundings seems to be involved in their emotion; some material circumstance suddenly appears to be strangely appropriate, appropriate even by its very incongruousness, to their stress of soul; their emotion seems to flow out and crystallize about this circumstance, so that for ever after the circumstance has the power of summoning up and recreating the emotion by which it was once touched. It gives to that emotion a preciseness which is never possessed by emotions which did not find their symbol.' [4]

It is the absence of this fusion that makes the wind on the heath irrelevant to Eustacia Vye, while its presence gives relevance and emotional force to a sound that she *was* listening for — the plop of a stone into the water, that told of Wildeve's coming. It is the constant presence of this fusion that enabled Flaubert, as exquisite a descriptive artist as Hardy, and an infinitely greater novelist, to provide a beautiful and significant background to Emma Bovary, a person who was really not much unlike Eustacia, and whose loves were just as ignoble. Flaubert, concentrating his thought and feeling on his character, was able to give in his background that beauty which her sordid story would otherwise lack, without ever for a minute diminishing our interest in that story, but on the contrary, heightening its intensity with every sight and sound.

'The soft night was about them, masses of shadow filled the branches. Emma, her eyes half-closed, breathed in with deep sighs the fresh wind that was blowing. They did not speak, lost as they were in the rush of their reverie. The tenderness of the old days came back to their hearts, full and silent as the flowing river, with the softness and perfume of the syringas, and threw across their memories shadows more immense and more sombre than those of the still willows that lengthened out over the grass. Often some night animal, hedgehog or weasel, setting out on the hunt, disturbed the lovers, or sometimes they heard a ripe peach falling all alone from the espalier.

"Ah! what a lovely night!" said Rodolphe.

"We shall have others," replied Emma.'

Or this passage:

'Once, during a thaw, the bark of the trees in the yard was oozing, the snow on the roofs of the outbuildings was melting; she stood on the threshold, and went to fetch her sunshade and opened it. The sunshade, of silk of the colour of pigeons' breasts, through which the sun shone, lighted up with shifting hues the white skin of her face. She smiled under the tender warmth, and drops of water could be heard falling one by one on the stretched silk.'

Or this:

'They returned to Yonville by the water-side. In the warm season the bank, wider than at other times, showed to its base the garden walls, whence a few steps led to the river. It flowed noiselessly, swift and cold to the eye; long, thin grasses huddled together in it as the current drove them, and spread themselves upon the limpid water like streaming hair; sometimes at the top of the reeds or on the leaf of a water-lily an insect with fine legs crawled or rested. The sun pierced with a ray the small blue bubbles of the waves that, breaking, followed each other; branchless old willows mirrored their grey backs in the water; beyond, all around, the meadows seemed empty. It was the dinner-hour at the farms, and the young woman and her companion heard nothing as they walked but the fall of their steps on the earth of the path, the words they spoke, and the sound of Emma's dress rustling round her.

The walls of the gardens with pieces of bottle on their coping were hot as the glass windows of a conservatory. Wallflowers had sprung up between the bricks, and with the tip of her open sunshade Madame Bovary, as she passed, made some of their faded flowers crumble into a yellow dust, or a spray of overhanging honeysuckle and clematis caught in its fringe and dangled for a moment over the silk.

They were talking of a troupe of Spanish dancers who were expected shortly at the Rouen theatre.

"Are you going?" she asked.

"If I can," he answered.

Had they nothing else to say to one another? Yet their eyes were full of more serious speech, and while they forced themselves to find trivial phrases, they felt the same languor stealing over them both.'

These passages, incomparably beautiful in the original, defy but survive translation, and show up Hardy's clod-hopping effects in comparison. One is temped to think only two kinds of background tolerable: Yonville or Highbury.

§ 7 'COUNTRIES OF THE MIND': JANE AUSTEN'S SATIRE

As well as the setting in which characters physically live and act, there are countries of the mind, places where their hearts and minds are present, in memory, fear, hope or desire — they carry about with them this second background, an effect too subtle for the stage, though the novelist may wish to avail himself of it.

Jane Austen, with her common-sense attitude to life, made a satirical use of the world of fantasy. Two of her descriptive scenes stand out by reason of their 'internal compulsion', but they are both scenes where a character is being mocked for not living in the actual but in a fantastic world. They have the flavour of her juvenile parodies, and one is inclined to think that they date from the earlier recensions of the novels in which they occur. If that is so, their vivacity no doubt earned their preservation, and we may be glad of it.

'My stupid sister has mistaken all your clearest expressions,' says Henry Tilney to Catherine Morland. 'You talked of expected horrors in London; and instead of instantly conceiving as any rational creature would have done, that such words could relate only to a circulating library, she immediately pictured to herself a mob of three thousand men assembling in St. George's Fields; the Bank attacked, the Tower threatened, the streets of London flowing with blood, a detachment of the 12th Light Dragoons (the hopes of the nation) called up from Northampton to quell the insurgents, and the gallant Captain Frederick Tilney, in the moment of charging at the head of his troop, knocked off his horse by a brick-bat from an upper window. Forgive her stupidity. The fears of the sister have added to the weakness of the woman; but she is by no means a simpleton in general.'

We may compare this with a mental picture from *Pride and Prejudice*.

'In Lydia's imagination, a visit to Brighton comprised every possibility of earthly happiness. She saw, with the creative eye of fancy, the streets of that gay bathing-place covered with officers. She saw herself the object of attention to tens and scores of them at present unknown. She saw all the glories of the camp — its tents stretched forth in beauteous uniformity of lines, crowded with the young and the gay, and dazzling with scarlet; and, to complete the view, she saw herself seated beneath a tent tenderly flirting with at least six officers at once.'

§8 BACKGROUND IN VIRGINIA WOOLF: KALEIDOSCOPIC

We do not live wholly either in the physical world, or in some country of the mind, evoked by memory, fear, hope, or desire. Mrs. Woolf, and other writers, who have followed the 'association of ideas' or the 'stream of consciousness', have provided a kaleidoscopic background for their characters: they live in several worlds at once.

Here is Septimus Warren Smith, in *Mrs. Dalloway*: 'lying on the sofa in the sitting-room; watching the watery gold glow and fade with the astonishing sensibility of some live creature on the roses, on the wall-paper. Outside the trees dragged their leaves like nets through the depths of the air; the sound of water was in the room, and through the waves came the voices of birds singing. Every power poured its treasures on his head, and his hand lay there on the back of the sofa, as he had seen his hand lie when he was bathing, floating, on the top of the waves, while far away on shore he heard dogs barking and barking far away. Fear no more, says the heart in the body, fear no more.'

And it is not only in the moment of drowning that our past life swims before our eyes, not only in moments of great emotional tension that we say: 'I shall never forget this.' In a trivial, boring moment the mind may suddenly decide to focus in this way, and an indelible picture is printed on the memory. It is in the reproduction of such moments that Virginia Woolf is a unique artist. Since they are rare, one may choose one of her humorous pictures to look at: an academic luncheon-party from *Jacob's Room*.

'Mr. Plumer got up and stood in front of the fireplace, Mrs. Plumer laughed like a straightforward friendly fellow. In short, anything more horrible than the scene, the setting, the prospect, even the May garden being afflicted with chill sterility and a cloud choosing that moment to cross the sun, cannot be imagined.'

It is humorous, certainly, but the horror is real — any reader who has had experience of such a scene will feel his blood run cold.

§ 9 THE UPHOLSTERY OF GALSWORTHY, CONTRASTED WITH HENRY JAMES

How crude in comparison is the descriptive writing of those novelists who tackle the problem of character presentation in the reverse way, not looking, as Mrs. Woolf does, at the external world through the eyes of the soul, with its complicated double and treble vision, but describing the town, then the street, then the house, then the room, then the clothes, and then the body that enclose the soul. They hope they have got their net so tightly round the soul itself that it cannot escape them, but it always does.

Mrs. Woolf herself attacked Bennett, Galsworthy and H. G. Wells for this practice. It can hardly be better illustrated than from *The Forsyte Saga*. Each Forsyte, or group of Forsytes, is built up from the background; we learn to know them apart by their furniture or their food. Old Jolyon has a study 'full of dark-green velvet and heavily carved mahogany', and when he gives a family dinner the saddle of mutton, the Forsyte *pièce de resistance*, is from Dartmoor. Swithin has an 'elaborate group of statuary in Italian marble, which placed upon a lofty stand (also of marble), diffused an atmosphere of culture throughout the room'. His mutton is Southdown. Soames 'inhabited a house which did what it could. It owned a copper door-knocker of individual design, windows which had been altered to open outwards, . . . and at the back (a great feature) a little court tiled with jade-green tiles, and surrounded by pink hydrangeas in peacock-blue tubs.' Soames belonged to the younger generation of Forsytes, who were tired of saddle of mutton, and had something else for dinner.

This is not at all a clear way of distinguishing character. We are expressly told that Soames's house had no real originality, but was like a great many others. If you collected and multi-plied traits of the kind Galsworthy has here given, you might in the end arrive at some slight discrimination of character. But it is obvious that this is an extremely laborious way of doing things. One ought rather to deduce from the character of any Forsyte, if he had been well drawn, what sort of furniture he would be likely to have, and what he would be likely to offer one if one dined with him — if it is really a matter of interest to know. But conjecture of this sort has more to do with pencil-and-paper games, and 'literary' competitions than with liter-ature.

The careful upholstery of Galsworthy is in striking contrast with the methods of Henry James, who, if ever a novelist had an excuse for detailed furnishing of a fictitious house, had such an excuse provided by the plot of *The Spoils of Poynton*. Yet we are told very little about the beautiful Poynton, we know only that there were double doors throughout, that there were precious tapestries, that there was a crucifix from Malta which was one of the best 'pieces'. However, Mrs. Gereth and Fleda are built up in our minds as persons of exquisite taste: they worship Poynton, so of course it must be exquisite.[5]

Waterbath, the Hell of vulgarity and ugliness, whence Mona Brigstock issues to threaten the Paradise of Poynton, is made real to us, guaranteed in exactly the same way — a week-end there made both Mrs. Gereth and Fleda cry. Otherwise its atrocities are left mercifully vague: 'The house was perversely full of souvenirs of places even more ugly than itself, and of things it would have been a pious duty to forget. The worst horror was the acres of varnish, something advertised and smelly with which everything was smeared: it was Fleda Vetch's conviction that the application of it, by their own hands and hilariously shoving each other, was the amusement of the Brigstocks on rainy days.'

§ 10 BACKGROUND: SEEN OBJECTIVELY AND SUBJECTIVELY

When all is said and done, there are only two ways of looking at the background in a novel. If it is looked at objectively, it must be seen only in so far as it explains the action, like scenery in a play. The piling up of details for their own sake is tedious and irrelevant.

The subjective view of the background is only legitimate when it is the view of one of the characters; there is no excuse for the author's subjective view, except perhaps when he enters into the story as Chorus, in the capacity of Time and Fate. Dickens is present in such a capacity when he evokes the rain in Lincolnshire, the fog of the Law Courts, or other of his symbolic atmospheres.

It would be said, no doubt, in justification of Hardy, that he is likewise present on the scene as the representative of Destiny. The artistic objections to Egdon Heath are, firstly, that Hardy the countryman forgets his function as representative of Destiny when he loads his picture with details of observation — for example about the different sounds made by the wind. Next, that when Hardy remembers he is the representative of Destiny, the Destiny he represents is so vast and crushing that his characters become trivial pygmies in comparison — they cannot stand up to Egdon Heath.

BACKGROUND

The backgrounds that are satisfying in fiction are the unemotional backgrounds of Miss Austen's novels — (though she can, when she pleases, paint landscape subjectively: Elinor looks at it with Sense, Marianne with Sensibility); the grand symbolic backgrounds of Dickens; Yonville, penetrated with the emotions of Emma Bovary. The sounds we continue to hear in the memory are the splash of Wildeve's stone into the water, the thud of the ripe peach in *Madame Bovary*, the dog in *Mrs. Dalloway*, 'far away barking and barking'.

NOTES

1. *English Prose Style* (1937), p. 118.
2. loc. cit., p. 71.
3. *Les Jeunes Filles*, p. 110. cf. Proust: 'Le cadre social, le cadre de la nature, qui entoure nos amours, nous n'y pensons presque pas. La tempête fait rage sur la mer, le bateau tangue de tous côtés, du ciel se précipitent des avalanches tordues par le vent et tout au plus accordons-nous une seconde d'attention pour parer à la gêne qu'elle nous cause, à ce décor immense où nous sommes si peu de chose, et nous et le corps que nous essayons d'approcher.' *Le Temps Retrouvé*, I, pp. 192-3.
4. cit. Denys Thompson: *Reading and Discrimination*, pp. 50-1.
5. Henry James has been rewarded, and Poynton is timelessly beautiful — changes of taste leave it unaffected. If he had described it, it might have been a disaster. I am informed by Miss Margaret Jourdain, than whom there can be no greater authority, that the illustrations he permitted to appear for *The Spoils of Poynton* suggest that, as he visualized it, it was perfectly hideous.

APPENDICES

I

'CLASSICAL PLACES'

It seems convenient to append here certain passages that may be
called '*loci classici*' for the novelist's art, statements of experience or
principle that have found no suitable place elsewhere in this treatise.
They are not offered as a coherent body of doctrine, but for what
they are: 'places'. It will not therefore at all matter if there should
happen to be contradictions between them.

The Novelist's Pains
PROUST

On peut presque dire que les œuvres comme dans les puits
artésiens, montent d'autant plus haut que la souffrance a plus
profondement creusé le cœur.

Le Temps Retrouvé, II, 66.

Les années heureuses sont les années perdues, on attend une
souffrance pour travailler. L'idée de la souffrance préalable s'associe
à l'idée du travail, on a peur de chaque nouvelle œuvre en pensant
aux douleurs qu'il faudra supporter d'abord pour l'imaginer. Et
comme on comprend que la souffrance est la meilleure chose que
l'on puisse rencontrer dans la vie, on pense sans effroi, presque
comme à une délivrance à la mort.

ibid., p. 68.

Certes, nous sommes obligés de revivre notre souffrance particu-
lière avec le courage du médecin qui recommence sur lui-même la
dangereuse piqûre.

ibid., p. 62.

C'est souvent seulement par manque d'esprit créateur qu'on ne
va pas assez loin dans la souffrance.

Sodome et Gomorrhe, III, p. 216.

FLAUBERT

(Writing to another novelist, whose wife was fatally ill): Tu
as et tu vas avoir de *bons* tableaux et tu pourras faire de *bonnes*
études! C'est chèrement les payer. Les bourgeois ne se doutent

guère que nous leur serrons notre cœur. La race des gladiateurs n'est pas morte, tout artiste en est un. Il amuse le public avec ses agonies.

Correspondance, III, p. 170.

CONRAD

And it is thus, with poignant grief in my heart, that I write novels to amuse the English.

Joseph Conrad: Life and Letters, by G. Jean Aubry (1927) I, p. 235.

The Novelist's Vocation
PROUST

Que celui qui pourrait écrire un tel livre serait heureux, pensais-je; quel labeur devant lui. Pour en donner une idée, c'est aux arts les plus élevés et les plus différents qu'il faudrait emprunter des comparaisons; car cet écrivain qui d'ailleurs pour chaque caractère aurait à en faire apparaître les faces les plus opposées, pour faire sentir son volume comme celui d'un solide, devrait préparer son livre, minutieusement, avec de perpétuels regroupements de forces, comme pour une offensive, le supporter comme une fatigue, l'accepter comme une règle, le construire comme une église, le suivre comme un régime, le vaincre comme un obstacle, le conquérir comme une amitié, le suralimenter comme un enfant, le créer comme un monde, sans laisser de côté ces mystères qui n'ont probablement leur explication que dans d'autres mondes et dont le pressentiment est ce qui nous émeut le plus dans la vie et dans l'art.

Le Temps Retrouvé, II, 239-40.

CONRAD

You must give yourself up to emotions (no easy task). You must squeeze out of yourself every sensation, every thought, every image, — mercilessly, without reserve and without remorse: you must search the darkest corners of your heart, the most remote recesses of your brain, — you must search them for the image, for the glamour, for the right expression. And you must do it sincerely, at any cost: you must do it so that at the end of your day's work you should feel exhausted, emptied of every sensation and every thought, with a blank mind and an aching heart, with the notion that there is nothing, — nothing left in you. To me it seems that it is the only way to achieve true distinction — even to go some way towards it.

loc. cit., I, p. 183.

Forethought

TROLLOPE

When we were young we used to be told, in our house at home, that 'elbow-grease' was the one essential necessary to getting a tough piece of work well done . . . Forethought is the elbow-grease which a novelist, — or a poet, or dramatist, — requires. It is not only his plot that has to be turned and re-turned in his mind, not his plot chiefly, but he has to make himself sure of his situations, of his characters, of his effects, so that when the time comes for hitting the nail he may know where to hit it on the head . . . It is from want of this special labour more frequently than from intellectual deficiency, that the tellers of stories fail so often to hit their nails on the head. To think of a story is much harder work than to write it. The author can sit down with the pen in his hand for a given time, and produce a certain number of words. That is comparatively easy, and if he have a conscience in regard to his task, work will be done regularly. But to think it over as you lie in bed, or walk about, or sit cosily over your fire, to turn it all in your thoughts, and make the things fit, — that requires elbow-grease of the mind. The arrangement of the words is as though you were walking simply along a road. The arrangement of your story is as though you were carrying a sack of flour while you walked.

Thackeray (English Men of Letters), ch. v.

Dryness

GIDE

Il arrive toujours un moment, et qui précède d'assez près celui de l'exécution, où le sujet semble se dépouiller de tout attrait, de tout charme, de toute atmosphère, même il se vide de toute signification, au point que, désépris de lui, l'on maudit cette sorte de pacte secret par quoi l'on a partie liée, et qui fait que l'on ne peut plus sans reniement s'en dédire. N'importe! on voudrait lâcher la partie. . . .

Je dis: 'on' mais après tout, je ne sais si d'autres éprouvent cela. Etat comparable sans doute à celui du catéchumène, qui, les derniers jours, et sur le point d'approcher de la table sainte, sent tout à coup sa foi défaillir et s'épouvante du vide et de la sécheresse de son cœur.

Journal des Faux-Monnayeurs.

CONRAD

And yet perhaps those days without a line, nay, without a word, the hard, atrocious, agonizing days are simply part of my *method* of work, a decreed necessity of my production.

loc. cit., II, p. 33.

Inspiration
CONRAD

One felt like walking out of a forest on to a plain — there was not much to see but one had plenty of light ... All of a sudden I felt myself stimulated. And then ensued in my mind what a student of chemistry would best understand from the analogy of the addition of the tiniest little drop of the right kind, precipitating the process of crystallization in a test-tube containing some colourless solution.

Preface to *The Secret Agent.*

KATHERINE MANSFIELD

It was a little café and hideous, with a black marble top to the counter, *garni* with lozenges of white and orange. Chauffeurs and their wives and fat men with immense photographic apparatus sat in it. And a white fox-terrier bitch, thin and eager, ran among the tables. Against the window beat a dirty French flag, fraying out on the wind and then flapping on the glass. Does black coffee make you drunk, do you think? I felt quite enivrée ... and could have sat three years, smoking and sipping and thinking and watching the flakes of snow. And then you know the strange silence that falls upon your heart — the same silence that comes one minute before the curtain rises. I felt that and knew that I should write here. ...

Letters of Katherine Mansfield, I, p. 9.

FLAUBERT

Il faut se méfier de tout ce qui ressemble à l'inspiration et qui n'est souvent que du parti pris et une exaltation factice que l'on s'est donnée volontairement et qui n'est pas venue d'elle-même; d'ailleurs on ne vit pas dans l'inspiration; Pégase marche plus souvent qu'il ne galope, tout le talent est de savoir lui faire prendre des allures qu'on veut, mais pour cela ne forçons point ses moyens, comme on dit en équitation, il faut lire, méditer beaucoup, toujours penser au style et faire le moins qu'on peut, uniquement pour calmer l'irritation de l'idée qui demande à prendre une forme et qui se retourne en nous jusqu'à ce que nous lui en ayons trouvé une, exacte, précise. . . .

Correspondance, I, pp. 186-7.

MEREDITH

. . . The best fiction is the fruit of a well-trained mind. If hard study should kill your creative effort, it will be no loss to the world or you.

Letters of George Meredith, I, p. 163.

Agonizing
SAMUEL BUTLER

Never consciously agonize; the race is not to the swift, nor the battle to the strong. Moments of extreme issue are unconscious and must be left to take care of themselves. During conscious moments take reasonable pains but no more and, above all, work so slowly as never to get out of breath. Take it easy, in fact, until forced not to do so.

There is no mystery about art. Do the things that you can see, they will show you those that you cannot see. By doing what you can you will gradually get to know what it is that you want to do and cannot do, and so be able to do it.

Note-Books.

Creation of Character
PROUST

Les gens du monde se représentent volontiers les livres comme une espèce de cube, dont une face est enlevée, si bien que l'auteur se dépêche de 'faire entrer' dedans les personnes qu'il rencontre.

Sodome et Gomorrhe, I, p. 53.

Ce sont nos passions qui esquissent nos livres, le repos d'intervalle qui les écrit. Quand l'inspiration renaît, quand nous pouvons reprendre le travail, la femme qui posait devant nous pour un sentiment ne nous le fait déjà plus éprouver. Il faut continuer à la peindre d'après une autre et si c'est une trahison pour l'autre, littérairement, grâce à la similitude de nos sentiments qui fait qu'une œuvre est à la fois le souvenir de nos amours passées et la péripetie de nos amours nouvelles, il n'y a pas grand inconvénient à ces substitutions. C'est une des causes de la vanité des études où on essaye de deviner de qui parle un auteur.

Le Temps Retrouvé, II, pp. 65-6.

APPENDICES

Conviction is found for others, — not for the author, only in certain contradictions and irrelevancies to the general conception of character (or characters) and of the subject. Say what you like, man lives in his eccentricities (so called) alone. They give a vigour to his personality which mere consistency can never do. One must explore deep and believe the incredible to find the few particles of truth floating in an ocean of insignificance. And before all one must divest oneself of every particle of respect for one's character.

Life and Letters, I, p. 301.

In a book you should love the idea and be scrupulously faithful to your conception of life. There lies the honour of the writer, not in fidelity to his personages. You must never allow them to decoy you out of yourself. As against your people you must preserve an attitude of perfect indifference, the part of creative power. A creator must be indifferent; because directly the 'Fiat!' has issued from his lips, there are the creatures made in his image that'll try to drag him down from his eminence, — and belittle him by their worship.

ibid., pp. 301-2.

Il m'est certainement plus aisé de faire parler un personnage, que de m'exprimer de mon nom propre; et ceci d'autant que le personnage créé diffère de moi davantage. Je n'ai rien écrit de meilleur ni avec plus de facilité que les monologues de Lafcadio, ou que le journal d'Alissa. Ce faisant, j'oublie qui je suis, si tant est que je l'aie jamais su. Je deviens l'autre ... Pousser l'abnégation jusqu'a l'oubli de soi total.

Journal des Faux-Monnayeurs.

Le mauvais romancier construit ses personnages; il les dirige et les fait parler. Le vrai romancier les écoute et les regarde agir; il les entend parler dès avant de les connaître.

ibid.

Observation

La tendance centrifuge, objective des hommes qui les pousse à abdiquer, quand ils goûtent l'esprit des autres, les sévérités qu'ils auraient pour le leur, et à observer, à noter précieusement, ce qu'ils dédaigneraient de créer.

La Prisonniére, II, p. 123.

C'est que dans l'état d'esprit où l'on 'observe' on est très audessous du niveau où l'on se trouve quand on crée.

A l'Ombre des Jeunes Filles en Fleurs, III, p. 8.

Recreation of Experience in the Imagination
HENRY JAMES

No such process is *effectively* possible, we must hold, as the imputed act of transplanting ... We can surely account for nothing in the novelist's work that hasn't passed through the crucible of his imagination, hasn't, in that perpetually simmering cauldron his intellectual *pot-au-feu*, been reduced to savoury fusion. We here figure the morsel, of course, not as boiled to nothing, but as exposed, in return for the taste it gives out, to a new and richer saturation ... Its final savour has been constituted, but its prime identity destroyed ... Thus it has become a different, and, thanks to a rare alchemy, a better thing. Therefore let us have here as little as possible about its 'being' Mr. This or Mrs. That. If it adjusts itself with the least truth to its new life it can't possibly be either.

The Art of the Novel, p. 230.

'Width of Range'
PROUST

Les niais s'imaginent que les grosses dimensions des phénomènes sociaux sont une excellente occasion de pénétrer plus avant dans l'âme humaine; ils devraient au contraire comprendre que c'est en descendant en profondeur dans une individualité qu'ils auraient chance de comprendre ces phenomènes.

Du Côté de Guermantes, II, p. 22.

Life and Fiction
JULIEN GREEN

Quel bizarre romancier que la vie! Comme elle repète ses effets, comme elle appuie de sa lourde main, comme elle écrit mal! Ou bien, elle revient sur ce qu'elle a dit, elle oublie le plan qu'elle avait en tête, elle se trompe de destinée et donne à l'un ce qui devait échoir a l'autre, elle rate le livre qu'elle tire à des millions d'exemplaires. Et tout à coup, de magnifiques éclairs de génie, des revirements, comme Balzac n'en rêva jamais, une audace de fou inspiré qui justifie toutes les erreurs et tous les tâtonnements.

Journal, Nov. 27th, 1932.

APPENDICES

Choice of Subjects
SAMUEL BUTLER

Do not hunt for subjects, let them choose you, not you them. Only do that which insists upon being done and runs right up against you, hitting you in the eye until you do it. This calls you and you had better attend to it, and do it as well as you can. But till called in this way do nothing.

Note-Books.

PROUST

(The narrator is here speaking to Albertine) Il est possible que les créateurs soient tentés par certaines formes de vie qu'il n'ont pas personellement éprouvées. Si je viens avec vous â Versailles . . . je vous montrerai le portrait de l'honnête homme par excellence, du meilleur des maris, Choderlos de Laclos, qui a écrit le plus effroyablement pervers des livres, et juste en face celui de Madame de Genlis qui écrivit des contes moraux et ne se contenta pas de tromper la duchesse d'Orléans, mais la supplicia en détournant d'elle ses enfants.

La Prisonnière, II, p. 240.

'Representation'
HENRY JAMES

The novelist who doesn't represent, and represent 'all the time' is lost, exactly as much lost as the painter who, at his work and given his intention, doesn't paint all the time.

loc. cit., p. 94.

Working out economically almost anything is the very life of the art of representation; just as the request to take on trust, tinged with the least extravagance, is the very death of the same.

ibid., p. 224.

The Pleasure of Writing
PROUST

Ecrire est pour un écrivain une fonction saine et nécessaire dont l'accomplissement rend heureux, comme pour les hommes physiques, l'exercice, la sueur et le bain.

Le Temps Retrouvé, II, p. 57.

The Writer's Duty
PROUST

Dès le début de la guerre, M. Barrès avait dit que l'artiste . . . doit avant tout servir la gloire de sa patrie. Mais il ne peut la servir qu'en

136

étant artiste, c'est-à-dire qu'à condition au moment où il étudie les
lois de l'Art . . . de ne pas penser à autre chose — fût-ce la patrie —
qu'à la vérité qui est devant lui.

ibid., p. 38.

The Christian Novelist

Profero etiam Domine (si digneris propitius intueri), tribulationes
plebium, pericula populorum, captivorum gemitus, miserias
orphanorum, necessitates peregrinorum, inopiam debilium, desper-
ationes languentium, defectus senum, suspiria iuvenum, vota
virginum, lamenta viduarum.

Roman Missal.

THE 'HALLUCINATION' THEORY OF
THE TURN OF THE SCREW

THE 'hallucination' theory of *The Turn of the Screw* is best known in the discussion of it by Mr. Edmund Wilson in *The Triple Thinkers*, though he disclaims having originated it. He states it as follows: 'according to this theory, the young governess who tells the story is a neurotic case of sex repression; and the ghosts are not real ghosts at all but merely the hallucinations of the governess.' This theory has been argued with such persuasiveness that it is time to refute it, and it can be refuted both by internal and external evidence.

Mr. Wilson analyses the story at length, in the interests of his theory, and it will be well to provide an analysis of the story on its face-value.

In the prologue one Douglas introduces the governess's manuscript. He makes it clear that he completely believes in her story, and regards her as a person of the greatest distinction of mind and character. She is the daughter of a clergyman; in answer to an advertisement she comes up to London, and is offered a post by a rich, young bachelor who wants a governess for his orphaned niece and nephew. The conditions attached to the post are that she is to take complete responsibility, and never bother the guardian about his wards. She accepts; it is admitted that she has fallen in love with her employer. She goes to Bly, his house in Essex, where Flora, the little girl, has been left with the housekeeper, Mrs. Grose, and some servants.

She learns that the boy, Miles, has been expelled from his school: no reason is given. She also learns from Mrs. Grose that the former governess, Miss Jessel, went away, and died: Mrs. Grose is obviously unwilling to pursue the subject.

In his analysis of this part of the story it is hard not to feel that Mr. Wilson has been slightly disingenuous, attempting to show the morbid mind of the governess. 'The boy, she finds, has been sent home from school for reasons into which she does not inquire but which she colours, on no evidence at all, with a significance somehow sinister . . . She learns that the former governess left, and that she has since died, under circumstances, which are not explained but which are made in the same way to seem ominous.'

After a period of halcyon days when the children are at their most charming, and when the governess thinks all that is needed to complete her felicity is the presence of their guardian, approving her endeavours for them, there comes a change 'actually like the spring of a beast'.

The figure of a man appears on one of the two towers of Bly, first taken by her for the master, and then seen obviously not to be he. Later he appears at the outside of a ground-floor window. She observes that he is wearing smart clothes, not his own. Mrs. Grose at once identifies the description: he is a valet of the master's, Peter Quint, who had once been in charge at Bly, and used to wear his master's clothes — Quint was dead. Mrs. Grose also reveals that he was a bad character, and that he was 'too free' with Miles, and 'too free' with everyone. The governess believes that he has come back to haunt the children, and that it is her duty to protect them.

Soon afterwards the governess is sitting by the side of the lake, and Flora is playing near her. She becomes aware of the presence of a third person on the other side of the lake. Flora has her back to the water: 'she had picked up a small flat piece of wood which happened to have in it a little hole that had evidently suggested to her the idea of sticking in another fragment that might figure as a mast and make the thing a boat. This second morsel, as I watched her, she was very markedly and intently attempting to tighten in its place.' She looks up and sees a handsome but evil woman in black, whom she concludes to be her predecessor. Mrs. Grose confirms that Miss Jessel was 'infamous', reveals that she had an affair with Quint, and implies that she went home to have a child by him, and died in consequence. The governess believes, encouraged in this belief by Mrs. Grose, that the children knew of and connived at the affair between Quint and Miss Jessel, and had been in some way corrupted by them; she further believes that they know that their dead friends haunt Bly.

At this point Mr. Wilson states, correctly, that there is no proof of anyone but the governess having seen the apparitions. He also calls attention to the Freudian imagery; the little girl's symbolic game with the pieces of wood, which so held the governess's gaze, and the first apparition of the male spectre on a tower, of the female behind a lake. These points will be considered later.

The only circumstance he admits as contradictory to his hypothesis that the ghosts are hallucinations, is the fact that the governess's description of the first ghost is identified by Mrs. Grose as Quint, of whom she has not yet heard. With great ingenuity he tries to show that she has built him up out of a chance hint from Mrs. Grose that

APPENDICES

there had been someone else in the place, other than the master, who 'liked every one young and pretty'. However, the description of Quint is so circumstantial that it cannot be so easily explained away. Furthermore, Miss Jessel is also seen distinctly before the governess has any details about her, and she is convinced of her 'infamy', although the worst Mrs. Grose had ever hinted was that she was not sufficiently 'careful' in some matters. Before her appearance behind the lake, nothing was known to her successor of Miss Jessel's affair with Quint: we are expressly told that there had been no servants' gossip. But the chief objection to the hallucination theory is the character of the governess herself, so carefully established in the prologue, and maintained throughout the story as that of a girl keeping her balance and courage in the most frightful circumstances.

After a second brief, halcyon period 'there suddenly came an hour' the narrator tells us, 'after which, as I look back, the affair seems to me to have been all pure suffering'. There is a third appearance of Quint, and the mysterious conduct of the children convinces the governess that they are in touch with the ghosts. 'They're his and hers ... Quint's and that woman's', she tells Mrs. Grose. 'They want to get to them.' Quint and Miss Jessel are coming back to keep the children safe for Evil. Mrs. Grose wants the governess to write to their uncle, but she decides that she must keep to her pledge that he is not to be bothered.

The children keep up the fiction that their uncle is coming to see them. Miles asks the governess when he is going to school again, and says that he will get his uncle to come down to Bly. This plunges her into an agony of indecision, and she is tempted to run away from the situation, but decides that she ought not to desert her post. Mr. Wilson states at this point: 'she is now apparently in love with the boy' — but this is not apparent on a natural reading of the text.

There follows the second appearance of Miss Jessel, and a curious manifestation in Miles's room where Mr. Wilson admits that the supernatural element can only be explained away by throwing doubt not only on the governess's explanation of her sensations, but on her record of the sensations themselves. 'She has felt a "gust of frozen air" and yet sees that the window is "tight". Are we to suppose she merely fancied that she felt it?' We shall see later the value of this admission.

Flora, having been lost, is found by the side of the lake. The governess for the first time names the ghost: 'Where, my pet, is Miss Jessel?' she asks. The dead governess appears, dreadfully, across the lake: 'she was there, so I was justified, she was there, so I was

140

neither cruel or mad.' (The first person to examine the 'hallucin-ation' theory is the governess herself.) Mrs. Grose does not see the apparition, and Flora denies that she sees it, turning in a violent reaction of hatred against the living governess. She continues in this state, and is sent up to London with Mrs. Grose.

Miles and the governess are left alone together. She presses him to tell her why he was expelled from school, and he confesses. He 'said' things — to 'a few', to those he liked, and they must have repeated them 'to those they liked'. 'It all sounds very harmless', is Mr. Wilson's extraordinary comment. It is hard to imagine anything more harmful: the little boy of innocent, even angelic appearance, with a mind filled with the abominations of Quint and Miss Jessel, spreading his dirty secrets round the school. In a moment the governess has seen an even more dreadful possibility: 'there had come to me out of my very pity the appalling alarm of his being perhaps innocent.' He might have been the innocent carrier of the germs of corruption, punished unjustly for carrying them.

This is the moment of the governess's victory, when Miles's soul is purged by confession, and there is complete confidence between them. Quint makes a last attempt against him; the boy does not see the apparition at the window, but the governess cries: 'No more, no more, no more!' 'Is she here?' asks the boy, and names Miss Jessel. Mr. Wilson comments, in direct contradiction to the text: 'He has, in spite of the governess's efforts, succeeded in seeing his sister and has heard from her of the incident at the lake.' We have Mrs. Grose's word, as well as the governess's that the children have not met — but Mr. Wilson is bound to go to this length if he is to keep his theory.

The governess says that it is not Miss Jessel. 'It's *he*?' asks Miles — whom does he mean by 'he?' she inquires. 'Peter Quint — you devil!'

She holds him in her arms, shows him the figure has vanished, he gives a cry, and dies in her arms. On the 'hallucination' theory she has frightened him to death. On a natural reading he dies, worn out by the struggle between good and evil, in the moment of triumph, like Morgan Moreen in *The Pupil*.

The 'hallucination' theory can then only be held:

(1) If we disbelieve Douglas's estimate of the governess's character.
(2) If we give a very strained explanation of her description of Quint.
(3) If we believe she is deluded about the very sense-data experi-enced in Miles's room, not only about her interpretation of them.

(4) If we believe, on no evidence, that Miles had got into touch with Flora after the scene by the Lake.

But the chief objection is one of general impression: this is not what the story means, and only perverted ingenuity, of a kind which has little to do with literature, could have detected the 'clue'. This is the ultimate answer to all such theories, from the Shakespeare-Bacon controversy to Verrall's brilliant perversities about Greek tragedy. Here there is a desire for a 'scientific' explanation, an unwillingness to make the necessary 'suspension of disbelief' in ghosts, which is completely opposed to the spirit in which the book should be read. It is only because Mr. Wilson is such a distinguished critic that the theory is worth further examination, and final refutation.

Mr. Wilson cites the preface to *The Turn of the Screw* as external proof of his theory.

(1) 'Peter Quint and Miss Jessel are not "ghosts" at all, as we now know the ghost, but goblins, elves, imps, demons as loosely constructed as those of the old trials for witchcraft.'

(2) Henry James speaks of 'our young woman's keeping crystalline her record of so many intense anomalies and absurdities — *by which I don't of course mean her explanation of them, a different matter . . .*' (Mr. Wilson's italics). Mr. Wilson says of the words in italics: 'These words seem impossible to explain except on the hypothesis of hallucination.'

But if we believe 'our young woman's' record of the actual happenings to be 'crystalline' clear, it is on that alone extremely difficult to accept the hypothesis of hallucination, as I have already shown. Moreover the preface itself shows us how we can doubt her explanation of the happenings, without supposing her to be the victim of hallucination. She clearly believes that she sees the spirits that once animated the earthly bodies of Quint and Miss Jessel; we can believe that she did indeed see *ab extra* apparitions, that another person with the right vision could have seen, without accepting her view of their eschatological status. They are not spirits of the dead, matter for psychical research, but 'goblins damned' — devils that have assumed the form of Quint and Miss Jessel to tempt the children. And this is surely the clear meaning of what Henry James says in the preface.

If Henry James was trying to hint in his preface that the ghosts were hallucinations, then he went about this in a very tortuous way; it seems rather that he has there alone provided enough evidence to discredit this theory. Yet Mr. Wilson writes: 'When we look back in the light of these hints, we become convinced that the whole story has been primarily intended as a characterization of the governess.' If this is what he really intended, then we can only explain Henry James's references to *The Turn of the Screw* in his letters on the hypothesis that he was a pathological liar.

As he nearly always did, Henry James began to construct this story not from a character, but from a scrap of anecdote. This scrap of anecdote had been told him by Archbishop Benson at Addington: 'the vaguest essence only was there — some dead servants and some children. This essence *struck* me and I made a note of it (of a most scrappy kind) on going home.'

On the character of the governess his letter to H. G. Wells is quite final: 'Of course I had, about my young woman to take a very sharp line. The grotesque business I had to make her picture and the childish psychology I had to make her trace and present, were, for me at least a very difficult job, in which absolute lucidity and logic, and a singleness of effect, were imperative. Therefore I had to rule out subjective complications of her own — play of tone, etc., and keep her impersonal save for the most obvious and indispensable little note of courage — without which she wouldn't have had her data.'

In short, the governess is the Jamesian observer or narrator, deliberately left *flou*, and only characterized up to the point which will make her observation plausible. The point of the story lies in the original anecdote told by the Archbishop.

Mr. Wilson argues that it lacks 'serious point' unless sex-frustration is the point; and he links it with Henry James's studies of spinsters in *The Bostonians* or *The Marriages*. But the affinity is surely rather with *The Pupil* or *What Maisie Knew*, those other studies of children isolated in an evil world. With *Maisie*, published in 1896, a year previous to *The Turn of the Screw*, the affinity is particularly close: that book ends with the rescue of a small child by a faithful governess from possible corruption at the hands of two immoral step-parents. Of *The Turn of the Screw* Henry James wrote to F. W. Myers: 'the thing I most wanted not to fail of doing, under penalty of extreme platitude, was to give the impression of the communication to the children of the most infernal imaginable evil and danger — the condition, on their part, of being as *exposed* as we can humanly conceive children to be.' This is surely a sufficiently serious point, and the fact that the details of the Evil are left to our imagination, links *The Turn of the Screw* with other stories of Henry James's where a secret is never revealed to the reader, e.g. *The Figure in the Carpet* and *Owen Wingrave*.

The data given by the Archbishop to Henry James were an old

house, and two children haunted by dead servants with the design of 'getting hold' of them. He has added a governess, a rich and handsome guardian, and an old housekeeper. Whence do these three figures derive? Probably from *Jane Eyre*. Jane Eyre went as governess to the orphaned ward of a rich bachelor (as she thought him), and had a housekeeper for company; she also was in love with her employer. When the first apparition of Quint is seen, the governess of *The Turn of the Screw* asks herself: 'Was there a "secret" at Bly — a mystery of Udolpho or an insane, an unmentionable relative kept in unsuspected confinement?' It is much to say that she had read *Jane Eyre* as well as *Udolpho*; the events of *The Turn of the Screw* are dated about the time of the publication of Charlotte Brontë's novel. But Henry James must have read *Jane Eyre*, and it is hard to resist the conviction that he was here thinking of the mad Mrs. Rochester. It is from literature rather than from the abnormal psychology of himself or his governess that the relation between her and the ghosts arises.

All that is left of the hallucination theory after close examination is the fact, on which it is based, of the sexual imagery of *The Turn of the Screw*: the man appears for the first time on a tower, wearing the clothes of his master, with whom the governess is in love; Miss Jessel appears for the first time behind a lake; Flora plays a symbolic game with pieces of wood — even the name of the story might be added. This is an interesting discovery, but it is dangerous to draw too many conclusions from it.

Mr. Stephen Spender makes the following comment in *The Destructive Element*: 'The only difficulty is that if the imagery were worked out consciously, it is hardly likely that James would have anticipated Freud with such precision. The horrible solution suggests itself that the story is an unconscious sexual fantasy, or that James has entered into the repressed governess's situation with an intuition that imposed on it a deeper meaning than he had intended.'

This is not, as we have seen 'the only difficulty'. And fortunately a solution can be found less distasteful than to call (however indirectly) a great writer a 'repressed governess'.

The sexual imagery is of a surface nature, the decoration of the story and not the story itself — it is giving it quite a disproportionate importance to call the story a 'sexual fantasy' on the strength of it — one might as well, on the strength of Miss Spurgeon's discoveries, say that *Romeo and Juliet* was a sun myth, because the dominating image in that play is Light.

The imagery in *The Turn of the Screw* one need hardly doubt comes rom the subconscious of an author, who was not aware of its sexual significance. Nor need that conclusion alarm us: let us consider what his conscious intelligence was at the moment triumphantly doing — it was making a great work of art out of a diabolically dirty story, treating the theme both with candour and with crystalline purity. If some unresolved elements lingering in the unconscious have found their resolution in the imagery, and have added to the total atmosphere of evil, it is only another illustration of the way that everything sometimes works together for good when a novelist is producing a great novel. If we are aware of the symbolism, and do not let it delude us, it adds to our appreciation of *The Turn of the Screw*.

Addendum. The recently published *Notebooks of Henry James* reveal that even the lake and the tower were implied in the Archbishop's story. The ghosts 'invite and solicit, the children 'from across dangerous places . . . so that the children may destroy themselves, lose themselves, by responding, by getting into their power'. Henry James adds: 'The story to be told — tolerably obviously — by an outside spectator, observer'. *The Notebooks of Henry James*, ed. F. O. Mathiessen and Kenneth B. Murdock (New York, 1947) pp. 178-9.

III

THE NOVELS OF I. COMPTON-BURNETT

A BRIEF BIBLIOGRAPHY

Dolores, 1911
Pastors and Masters, 1925
Brothers and Sisters, 1929
Men and Wives, 1931
More Women Than Men, 1933
A House and Its Head, 1935
Daughters and Sons, 1937
A Family and A Fortune, 1939
Parents and Children, 1941
Elders and Betters, 1944
A Conversation between I. Compton-Burnett and M. Jourdain (in *Orion: a miscellany*), 1945
Manservant and Maidservant, 1947

THE indebtedness of Miss Compton-Burnett to Jane Austen is generously acknowledged. It is the mark of one of her insincere or self-complacent characters that he does not much care for Jane Austen's novels.

'"What do you think of Miss Jane Austen's books, Jermyn," said Dominic, "if I may approach so great a man upon a comparatively flimsy subject?"

"Our row of green books with the pattern on the backs, Rachel?" said Sir Percy with a sense of adequacy in conversation. "Very old-fashioned, aren't they?"

"What do the ladies think of the author, the authoress, for she is of their own sex?" said Dominic.

"I have a higher standard for greatness," said Agatha, "but I don't deny she has great qualities. I give her the word great in that sense."

"You put that very well, Mrs. Calkin," said Dominic. "I feel I must become acquainted with the fair writer."'

THE NOVELS OF I. COMPTON-BURNETT

The world that the two novelists depict is normally a limited one, the families at the big house, the rectory, and one or two other houses in an English village. Their social world ranges from a baronet to a respectable upper servant. In *Pastors and Masters* Miss Compton-Burnett has drawn a very vivid picture of a preparatory-school, but in her women's college in *Dolores* or her girl's school in *More Women than Men* little more education is shown taking place than in Mrs. Goddard's school in *Emma*; she has chosen the school simply as an example, like the family, of a group of people living too closely together. The men in her books are doctors or clergy, or are present for long week-ends — having work in London and outside the books — or else they have retired from their professions, or never had any. 'Their professions and occupations are indicated', she says in the *Conversation*, 'but I am concerned with their personal lives; and following them into their professional world would lead to the alternations between two spheres, that I think is a mistake in books. I always regret it in the great Victorian novelists, though it would be hard to avoid it in books on a large scale.'

Why has she chosen this world, and why has she dated the action of her books some time between 1888 and 1902?[1]

Not out of a desire to imitate — Jane Austen is inimitable, and Miss Compton-Burnett has a very original mind. Nor has she acted out of nostalgia for a quiet, old-fashioned world: there is nothing quaint about her work, any more than there is about Miss Austen's — no period properties and no local colour.

She herself claims that she is accepting her limitations: 'I do not feel that I have any real or organic knowledge of life later than about 1910. I should not write of later times with enough grasp or confidence. I think this is why many writers tend to write of the past. When an age is ended, you see it as it is. And I have a dislike, which I cannot explain, of dealing with modern machinery and inventions. When war casts its shadow, I find that I recoil.'

Such a recognition of her range is in itself admirable, but it is impossible not to see more than that in the limitations within which she works. She is writing the pure novel, as Jane Austen did, concentrating upon human beings and their mutual reactions. So rare is such concentration in the English novel that any writer who conscientiously practises it is almost sure to be accused of 'imitating Jane Austen' whether their minds are alike or not: and the minds of Miss Austen and Miss Compton-Burnett are in many ways alike.

[1] The events of *Pastors and Masters* take place after 1918: this is the one exception.

147

APPENDICES

The isolation of her characters (and in all her novels except *Dolores* and *More Women Than Men* there is strict unity of place) brings them into clearer relief, and enables their creator to do her real business, the study and revelation of human nature, with greater freedom. This isolation of the characters, and their lack of interest in social conditions outside the family, or in economic problems apart from those of the family fortunes, is made more credible by isolating them in time as well as in place — situating them in a period when the impact of public events on private individuals was less immediate and crushing than at present. Therefore she has chosen the end of Queen Victoria's reign. A few years earlier, and she would have been obliged to weight down her books with the trappings of the historical novel: as it is, she has obtained a liberating absence of contemporaneity at the small cost of substituting carriages for cars.

As if to boast of her freedom, her references to Politics are deliberately and engagingly flat. 'So you see, Parliament thought that Bill a wrong one, and it was thrown out,' Mr. Burgess observes to one of his pupils in *Pastors and Masters*; and Duncan Edgeworth in *A House and its Head* asks: 'You don't think this election business will follow that course?'

Miss Compton-Burnett has freed herself from all irrelevances in order to write the pure novel. And like Miss Austen she has a dislike for merely descriptive writing, which she uses with even greater economy.[1] The village which is to be the scene of action is undescribed and, except for Moreton Edge in *Brothers and Sisters*, is not even named. Characters are often tersely but completely described, in terms which do not remain in the memory, and it is necessary to turn back if we wish to remind ourselves of their appearance.

'Duncan Edgeworth was a man of medium height and build, appearing both to others and himself to be tall. He had narrow, grey eyes, stiff, grey hair and beard, a solid, aquiline face, young for his sixty-six years, and a stiff, imperious bearing. His wife was a small, spare, sallow woman, a few years younger, with large, kind prominent eyes, a long, thin, questioning nose, and a harried, innocent, somehow fulfilled expression.'

One is inclined to wonder if much would be lost by the suppression of such passages. The author herself observes in the *Conversation*:

[1] She will introduce cushions, like an easily portable stage-property, as an emblem of prosperity. Peter (in *Brothers and Sisters*) spills his tea over Sophia's cushions. Sabine Ponsonby (in *Daughters and Sons*) puts out cushions only when visitors are expected. Hope Cranmer (in *Parents and Children*) has cushions, and the Marlowes haven't.

'I am sure that everyone forms his own conceptions, that are different from everyone else's, including the author's.'

Dialogue, to which in *Emma* Jane Austen had begun to give a far more important place, is the staple of this writer's work. It is a dialogue of a power and brilliance unmatched in English prose fiction. In her early and immature book, *Dolores*, the machine creaked audibly at times, but already functioned with precision. The style of that book is crude, bare and rather alarming. It is not like real English: it is like the language of translation. It reminds one of English translations of Russian novels and of Greek tragedy, and one may conjecture that both of them had formed an important part of her reading. Such a style is uneuphonious and harsh, but conscientiously renders a meaning — and that is what, like a translator, Miss Compton-Burnett already did, with a remarkable exactitude.

This ungainly, but precise language was later evolved into a dialogue, more dramatic than narrative, which, whether in longer speeches, or in the nearest equivalent in English to Greek tragic stichomythia, is an unrealistic but extraordinarily intense vehicle for the characters' thoughts and emotions, and enables their creator to differentiate them sharply, and, whenever she wishes, to condemn them out of their own mouths. Its nearness to or remoteness from ordinary spoken language will vary from place to place. There is no single formula that will cover it, and the author has indicated that no kind of 'figure in the carpet' is to be sought: 'it is simply the result of an effort to give the impression I want to give'.

'The key', says one critic, 'is the realization that her characters speak precisely as they are thinking.' This key will not unlock more than a part of her work: part of the utterances of her good characters, and the utterances of exceptionally simple or straightforward characters.

For she excels particularly at the revelation of insincerity on all its levels: from that of characters who tell flat lies, to that of characters who have deceived themselves into believing what they say. In between are characters such as Dominic Spong, who are more than half-aware and are wholly tolerant of their own smarminess and their own insincere ways of talking: 'if I may approach so great a man upon a comparatively flimsy subject.'

Her idiom sometimes approximates to what one might actually say if one were in the character's skin and situation, but also to what one might think and conceal; to what one might think of saying and bite back; to what one might afterwards wish one had said; to what one would like other people to think; and to what one would like to think oneself. It is unlikely that these alternatives are exclusive. A full analysis, with the necessary illustrations, would require the full-length book that should be written on Miss Compton-Burnett's work.

A resemblance to Jane Austen may be noted in the use of stilted or unmeaning language to indicate a bad or insincere character. The pretentious vulgarity of Mrs. Elton with her 'Caro Sposo' or 'Hymen's saffron robe', the frigid pomposity of Sir Edward Denham's thoughts on the Novel, or of General Tilney's compliments to Catherine Morland have frequent parallels — generally in the speech of characters who pride themselves on their superior sensitiveness, subtlety, public spirit, or culture.

A speech of Dulcia Bode in *A House and Its Head* contains many of the worst horrors pilloried by Fowler in *Modern English Usage*. Fowler shows that such faults are not merely faults of expression, but generally spring from real faults in feeling and character; they are not merely due to faulty taste, but to moral faults — insincerity, vanity, cowardice, and more.

' "Now, Mother dear, lift up your head and your heart. Mr. Edgeworth has not roused himself from his own shock and sorrow — yes, and shame; for it must be almost that — to point us in our direction, without looking for a touch of resilience and response. We can best repay him by throwing up our heads, facing the four winds squarely, and putting our best foot foremost out of the morass, and also out of his house." '

Here are BATTERED ORNAMENTS, HACKNEYED PHRASES, IRRELEVANT ALLUSION, MIXED METAPHOR and FACETIOUS ZEUGMA. Elsewhere in the utterances of this irrepressible character are POLYSYLLABIC HUMOUR ('I suspect I shall come by a good deal of refreshment in the course of my peregrinations'), SUPERIORITY ('if I may be Irish') and many other atrocities.

Dulcia, however, is not a mere Slipslop or Malaprop, but a very penetrating delineation of an unsubtle and insensitive nature given to uncontrolled self-dramatization, and to the dramatization of her environment. Many other characters betray themselves by their speech, and some in ways too subtle to be illustrated by a brief citation. This feature of her style, alone, would make Miss Compton-Burnett a most remarkable writer.

Besides the terse descriptions of characters there are a few short descriptions of action, or brief paragraphs of introduction or transition, such as the exquisitely phrased entrance of Miss Charity Marcon in *Daughters and Sons*.

'Miss Charity Marcon walked up her garden path, crossed her hall and entered her plain little drawing-room, her great height almost coinciding with the door, and her long neck bending, lest the experience of years should prove at fault and it should quite coincide with it.'

Since the short study *Pastors and Masters*, published in 1925 after a fourteen years' silence, Miss Compton-Burnett has been completely mistress of her unique style, which has she used in increasing perfection in the novels that have followed. The texture is so close and dramatic that quotation of isolated passages is almost impossible without leaving a misleading impression. The detachment by reviewers of some of her comic passages, which are the most easily quotable, has perhaps tended to give the impression that she is only a humorous writer, and to obscure the fact, intensely humorous though she often is, that her ironic view of family life is also serious, and even tragic.

Miss Austen drew family tyranny in two characters: General Tilney in *Northanger Abbey* and Mrs. Norris in *Mansfield Park*. After her time family life went into a darker period. Victorian parents (though there were charming people among them) sometimes identified themselves with God, and modelled their behaviour towards their children upon that of Jehovah towards the Children of Israel at their most recalcitrant — and they claimed divine authority for their worst excesses. Theobald and Christina in *The Way of All Flesh* are terrifying family tyrants: they are closely drawn from Samuel Butler's own parents. Novels of the period are full of fearful autocracy, approved by the Victorian authors. There are plenty of memoirs to substantiate the evidence with genuine atrocity stories. Even in our own century, when the bonds of family life have greatly relaxed, the domestic dictator still horribly flourishes. You would not believe what goes on behind the façade of many a comfortable family residence. Those whose own lives have been happy in this respect, are shocked and incredulous when they obtain an insight into the terrors of family life as it can be lived. As one of Miss Compton-Burnett's characters observes: 'people do not know about families.'

The subject-matter of all her books — tyranny in family life — is therefore neither unreal nor unimportant. On the contrary, it is one of the most important that a novelist could choose. The desire for domination, which in a dictator can plunge the world into misery, can here be studied in a limited sphere. The courage of those who resist dictation, and the different motives which cause people to range themselves on the side of the dictator can be minutely studied. In avoiding contemporary chatter about public events, Miss Burnett has gone instead to the heart of the matter:

her works provide one with more penetrating social criticism than all propagandist fiction put together. The moral is this — and it is both edifying and beautiful — if a novelist refuses to be seduced by the clamour of contemporary fashion into a dissertation upon economics, politics, the philosophy of history or the like, and if he is true to his calling, which is the study of human nature, then all these other things will be given to him. He will inevitably be a social critic, a philosopher of history.

In each of the novels there is a tyrant; family tyranny is always an important, usually the most important theme. In *Dolores* the selfish claims of Cleveland Hutton are always liable to break up the academic career which his daughter has made for herself — in this youthful book her self-sacrifice is regarded as noble: in the later books it would have been thought horrible. In *Pastors and Masters* Henry Bentley, another clergyman, makes his children the victims of his nervous depression. In *Brothers and Sisters* Sophia Stace, and in *Men and Wives* Harriet Haslam are tyrannical and devouring mothers, though they differ from each other in their aims and methods, and their mental make-up.

The following scene, between Sophia Stace, her children and their former nurse, on the evening after her husband's funeral, is one of the author's finest comic scenes, but it is merely comic only to those who are too insensitive to see that the family tyrant is as evil as the dictator, and ethically far less easily defensible.

' "I don't know whether you all like sitting there, having your dinner, with your mother eating nothing? On this day of all days! I don't know if you have thought of it."

"Oh, I understood that you wouldn't have anything," said Patty, rising and hurrying to her side with food. "I am sure I thought you said that."

"I may have said those words," said Sophia. "It is true that I do not want anything. I hardly could, could I? But I may need it. It may be all the more necessary for me, for that reason. I don't think I should be left without a little pressing to-day, sitting here, as I am, with my life emptied. I hardly feel you should let me depend quite on myself."

Her children's power of rising to such demand was spent. Patty pressed food with a simply remorseful face.

"No, I will not have anything," said Sophia, with her eyes on the things in a way that gave Dinah one of her glimpses of her mother as pathetic. "Nobody minds whether I do or not; and that would be the only thing that would persuade me, somebody's caring. I can't make the effort alone."

"Here, come, try some of this," said Dinah. "It is so light you can get it down without noticing."

"And this, and this," said Andrew, coming forward with a dish in each hand, and an air of jest.

"Darlings!" said Sophia, taking something from Dinah. "Dear ones! Yes, I will try to eat a little to please you. Let me have something from you, my Andrew. I will do my best." '

Josephine Napier, in *More Women Than Men*, is a more subtle type of tyrant, who is able to lead as well as drive her family and colleagues into obedience; she is the most attractive and the most dangerous of the tyrants, and the only one who combines that role with murder. Duncan Edgeworth, in *A House and Its Head*, has the superior honesty and directness of the male oppressor, but his oppression is the more open and ruthless. In *Daughters and Sons*, the matriarch, Sabine Ponsonby, and her unbalanced daughter, Hetta, both tyrannize over their household. In *A Family and A Fortune*, Matilda Seaton tries to tyrannize over her richer relations, and succeeds in making the life of her paid companion impossible. The tyranny of the grandfather, Sir Jesse Sullivan, in *Parents and Children*, and of the invalid aunt, Sukey Donne, in *Elders and Betters* come less in the middle of the picture of those two books, and yet are the cause of most of the happenings.

In most cases it is the economic dependence of other people upon them that enables the tyrants to exercise their shocking power — but this is not always the case. Some people who are not economically dependent submit to it, because they are bound in affection to others who are economically dependent, and therefore wish to live in the tyrant's house. And of course Miss Compton-Burnett is too subtle to accept the economic explanation as the only one. In some cases it has nothing to do with the question. Three of her tyrannical aunts hold no purse strings, and one of them is, on the contrary, a poor relation, a dependant — at any rate as far as extra comforts are concerned — on the family which she dominates by her will. Such was the position of Mrs. Norris in *Mansfield Park*.

Tyranny in the family generates a tense electric atmosphere in which anything might happen. Every thought, however outrageous, is given full and clear expression — for not only do the tyrants say exactly what they think, so, oddly, do their victims as well. The equivalent of the play-scenes in *Mansfield Park* are invested with the grimness of the play-scenes in *Hamlet*. A family conversation at the breakfast table is so pregnant with horror, that one feels things cannot go on like this for long; the storm must break some time. One is quite right, it does break. This may happen in one of two ways, but there will probably be violent happenings. It is the great distinction of Miss Compton-Burnett among highly civilized writers that her violence is always entirely credible.[1]

Violent action shakes up the characters in a novel, and it is foolish of writers to despise the strong situation: it may be most revealing about human behaviour. Mr. Forster says, with some justice, that in the domain of violent physical action Jane Austen is feeble and ladylike. Miss Compton-Burnett is neither: she comes serenely to violence like the great tragic artist that she is. She has so effectively prepared the way for it that when it inevitably comes, like war after a crisis, it is immediately felt to be a clearing of the air. The crime or adultery is seen to be less shocking than the daily cruelty at the breakfast table. After the violence has died down, the chief characters, completely revealed, and to some extent participating in the purge by pity and terror, which has been the lot of readers and minor characters alike, resume their old life rather more quietly, and everything is hushed up, though everyone knows.

The violent happenings are of two sorts, as in Greek tragedy: either there is a crime, or the discovery of something dreadful in the past. These respectable families, descendants it might be of Jane Austen's Bennets, Bertrams or Knightleys, have within them the same seeds of destruction as the houses of Oedipus or of Agamemnon. Those happenings in that setting produce the effect which Miss Elizabeth Bowen has well described as 'sinister cosiness'.

If we read the *faits divers* in the newspapers we are apt to find unexplained and mysterious happenings: sometimes we meet with them in our own circle of acquaintance. A devoted husband and wife suddenly separate; a brilliant boy is found hanging in his bedroom. We do not know why, but there are some people who know, and who will take care that we never know. How many more must be the happenings we know nothing of at all. 'I think there are signs that strange things happen, though they do not emerge', says Miss Compton-Burnett. 'I believe it would go ill with many of us, if we were faced by a strong temptation, and I suspect that with some of us it does go ill.'

She shows us how strange things happen — she really shows us how. She traces them from their roots in the characters of the people to whom they happen. Therefore there is no vulgar melodrama, no matter how sensational the happenings are.

In *Pastors and Masters*, a mainly humorous study, the crime is only

---

[1] The present writer must admit some difficulty in accepting the fraud in *Parents and Children*.

a fairly harmless literary forgery. In *Brothers and Sisters* it is found that Sophia Stace's husband was also her half-brother; and the secret of Christian Stace's parentage has caused other tangled relationships, which nearly become incestuous. The source of inspiration is again acknowledged. One of the characters remarks: 'We are beginning to leave off feeling branded, but all our friends seem shy of us. It is too like an ancient tragedy for them.'

In *Men and Wives*, Matthew Haslam poisons his domineering mother. In *More Women Than Men*, Josephine is morally, though not legally guilty of her nephew's wife's death. In *A House and Its Head*, Grant Edgeworth commits adultery with his uncle's second wife; their child is acknowledged as Duncan Edgeworth's son and heir, and is murdered by a servant at the instance of Sibyl, Grant's wife and Duncan's daughter, in order to remove the bar to Grant's inheritance of the family estate. In *Daughters and Sons* the crime is no more than a pretended (perhaps really attempted) suicide by Hetta Ponsonby. There is no crime or guilty secret in *A Family and A Fortune*, though two characters are driven to leave their homes sensationally in a snow-storm. Fraud of one sort or another is practised in *Parents and Children* and *Elders and Betters*: in the former it is dramatically unmasked, in the latter it remains triumphant — moreover the niece who has burnt one aunt's will drives another aunt to suicide.

The connection between tyranny and violence is generally causal. In *Men and Wives* the tyrant is the direct victim of the crime; in *More Women Than Men* and *Daughters and Sons* a tyrant, in the danger of losing power, commits the crime in an attempt to preserve her domination. In *A House and Its Head* the tense family atmosphere, caused by Duncan's tyranny, is itself the cause of Sibyl's lack of mental balance, and of her crime. In the last two books the causation is less immediate — but it is the tyranny of Sir Jesse Sullivan that encourages Ridley Cranmer to think that his daughter-in-law will do anything to get out of his house, even to the point of assenting to a bigamous marriage — and the tyranny of Sukey Donne makes possible Anna's fraudulent substitution of a will in which she disinherits those who have the first claim on her.

It is the mark of bad, stupid or insincere characters that they are wholly or partly on the tyrant's side, through weakness, cowardice, hope of personal profit, or through a conventional or sentimental veneration of the Family as an institution, and of the tyrant as the obvious head of a family. Harriet Haslam is toadied by her lawyer, Dominic Spong, and Sabine and Hetta Ponsonby by their clergyman, Dr. Chaucer. Most of the neighbours respect and over-indulge Duncan Edgeworth. It is only singularly acute people who avoid being taken in by Josephine Napier. The bad characters see virtues in the tyrants which have no objective existence; they do not dare to believe in the evil that is there, because they are too morally cowardly to take sides against it.

By contrast, and in themselves, the good characters are very good indeed. Where other novelists are often weak, Miss Compton-Burnett is strong, in the creation of likeable good characters. Her good people are intelligent and nice. They always have those qualities that we really most wish to find in our friends. Not that they are always conventionally irreproachable, though there is nothing to be said against Cassandra Jekyll in *A House and Its Head*, Helen Keats in *More Women Than Men*, or several others. 'I like good people,' says Maria Sloane in *A Family and A Fortune*. 'I never think people realize how well they compare with the others.'

The sex-life of Maria Rosetti, Felix Bacon and Grant Edgeworth has not been unblemished; Andrew, Dinah and Robin Stace, Evelyn Seymour, Terence Calderon and Dudley Gaveston are entirely idle; few of the good characters are particularly brave, most of them are irreligious, none of them are at all public-spirited — certainly they are not perfect. But they are serious, honest and sensitive, their human values are always right, and they will, if necessary, defend them. They never talk in slang or clichés; they never tell lies to others or to themselves about their feelings or motives — the bad characters think them unfeeling and selfish because they scorn pretence. They have virtues that are rare and unconventional: while many of the bad characters pride themselves on speaking good of everyone, the good characters know that it may be a higher form of charity to abuse tyrants to their victims, or to allow the victims the rare indulgence of speaking against their tyrants. The personal relations, whether of friendship or marriage or family affection, that subsist between the good characters, are as good as such relations can ever be, in life or in fiction. They are for Miss Compton-Burnett, as for Mr. Forster, the supreme value — and she vindicates them against worse dangers than anyone in his novels has to face. Her arms, however, are not mystical; it is by truth, affection and intelligence only that her good characters conquer — and the greatest of these is intelligence. No one in fact or fiction has, or deserves to have, more self-respect than they. 'He respects us,' says a woman in *Parents and Children* about the old tyrant Sir Jesse. 'Ah, how I respect us!' replies her brother.

In consequence of their character the utterances of the good people have a directness and ruthlessness with which no mere cynic could compete.

'Let us all speak with a lack of decent feeling,' says Dinah Stace. 'It is time we did something out of keeping with the dignity of bereavement. It is a bad kind of dignity.'

'Other people's troubles are what they deserve. Ah, how they deserve them!' says Oscar Jekyll.

'Are you of the stuff that martyrs are made of?' says Chilton Ponsonby to his sister France, who is in danger of submitting to parental tyranny. 'I hope not; it is useless stuff.'

'I suppose I shall subscribe to hospitals,' says Dudley Gaveston, on coming into his fortune. 'That is how people seem to give to the poor. I suppose the poor are always sick. They would be, if you think. I once went round the cottages with Edgar, and I was too sensitive to go a second time. Yes, I was too sensitive even to set my eyes on the things which other people actually suffered, and I maintain that that was very sensitive.'

'Self-knowledge speaks ill for people,' says Hope Cranmer. 'It shows they are what they are almost on purpose.'

'I feel that to know all is to forgive all,' says Terence Calderon, 'and other people seem to forgive nothing. And no one can say they don't know all. I have never thought of any way of keeping it from them.'

Nor are the tyrants themselves incapable of goodness. Some of them are even capable of acts of almost heroic virtue, following hard upon others of extreme baseness. Sophia Stace, Josephine Napier and Matilda Seaton, the most intelligent of them, have moments of inspired sympathy. Where angels might fear to tread, and where the *anima naturaliter Christiana*, if a simple soul, would be likely to blunder, they walk sure-footed. It is a truism that a good heart may often guide a poor head: they prove that the converse may also be true. In them a fine understanding can produce fine and generous behaviour; in certain subtle difficulties it would be to them that one would turn for support, sooner than to many better-hearted people. Their creator reminds us that Wisdom is, after all, an intellectual virtue, and that the children of this world can be wiser (and, so far, to be more commended) than the children of light.

Most of the tyrants receive and deserve some respect and affection, even from their victims: the tyranny never quite abolishes family feeling, and when a tyrant has a bad fall the victims are chivalrously ready to pick him up. Some of them secure friendship and deep affection from characters of complete integrity, who see their faults clearly, but are yet fond of them — and this friendship and affection is also at least in part deserved. The tyrants are never all bad, and therefore untragic. Their fate cannot be a matter of indifference; in the one instance of tyrannicide, in *Men and Wives*, the pity of Harriet's death is as moving as the horror of Matthew's crime.

The last scene between Matthew and his mother can hardly have been read by those who profess to find neither action nor passion in Miss Compton-Burnett's books. It is wonderfully eloquent, and shows that she has the distinction, unique among living English prose-writers, of being capable of tragedy.

'Matthew followed his mother upstairs, and was drawn by her into her room. "Matthew," she said, standing with her hand on his shoulder and her eyes looking up into his face, "I want you to do something for me; not a great thing dear; I would not ask that. I don't ask you to give up your work, or to give up your marriage; I know you cannot give up. I don't mean that any of us can; I am not saying anything to hurt. I only mean that I would not ask much of you. I just want you to put off your marriage for a few months, for your mother's sake, that she may have a little space of light before the clouds gather. I don't mean that my illness is coming again; I don't think it will come yet. And if it were, I would not use that to persuade you. I would not do what is not fair, while I am myself. I think you know I would not then. But I ask you simply, and as myself, to do this thing for me. I feel I can ask you, because I have seen your eyes on me tonight, and I have said to myself: 'My son does not love me, not my eldest son. And it is my fault, because mothers can easily be loved by their sons. So I can ask this from him, because I cannot lose his love, or lessen it. I have not put it in him.' And so I ask it of you, my dear."

"Mother, what a way to talk!" said Matthew. "Indeed your illness is not coming again. You could not be more at the height of your powers. Your speech was worth taking down. You may use it again. It was only I who heard it. My eyes show all this to you, when all my eyes are for Camilla at the moment, and if anyone knows that, it is you! I might tell you what your eyes show to me, and you would not have an answer. Now take one of your sleeping-tablets; I think I should take two; I have put them out on this table. And the marriage shall not happen until you sanction it. Camilla can get what she wants from this family, from you. She will have you as a friend before me as a husband. I daresay that will be the end."

Harriet stood with her eyes searching her son's.

He kissed her and left her, and turned from the door and gave her the smile that should safeguard for both of them this memory.'

It is not surprising that the only successful, living writer of English verse tragedy should show signs of Miss Compton-Burnett's influence both on the situation and the dialogue of *The Family Reunion* — though its action is more diffuse and less tragic than the greater moments in her novels. Perhaps it is not entirely fanciful to see Mr. Eliot acknowledging this influence when he names one of his characters Ivy, and gives another an invitation to stay at 'Compton-Smith's place in Dorset'.

The tragic aspects of Miss Compton-Burnett's work have been dwelt on at this length, because of their immense significance. They mark her divergence from Jane Austen, and her unique position and stature as a novelist, and they indicate the importance which she attaches to her implied view of life. Briefly, she holds with Mr. Forster that, to be good, people must be serious and truthful, and had better be intelligent; but she differs from him in adding that Charity begins at home. Her good and intelligent characters are not public-spirited, and her philanthropists are almost invariably prigs or bores, though delightfully entertaining.

Lydia Fletcher in *Pastors and Masters* has her men's class, her 'dear men things'. In *Men and Wives* there is an inimitable working-party. The village in *A House and Its Head* is cursed with three women, ruthlessly going about doing good to their neighbours.

For, like Miss Austen, Miss Compton-Burnett is a great comic writer.

'I am such a votary of the comic muse. "No," I have said, when people have challenged me, "I will not have comedy pushed into a back place." I think tragedy and comedy are a greater, wider thing than tragedy by itself. And comedy is so often seen to have tragedy behind it.'

This is true of her work, though it is an absurd character who says it. As well as humorously exploiting situations, and making use of epigrammatic brilliance in dialogue, she is a great creator of comic characters. Many of them play an active part as the philan-thropic busybodies or the tyrant's parasites, to whom reference has been made — roles which are often combined. Others, like Mrs. Christy who has just been quoted, have a more simply decorative function.

A scene from *Pastors and Masters* illustrates the simpler form of humour, rare in her later work, of several absurd characters in action together.

"Mrs. Merry," Miss Basden said, in a rather high monotone, "the boys are saying that the marmalade is watery. I am telling them that no water is used in marmalade, that marmalade does not contain water, so I do not see how it can be."

"I do not see how it can be, either; but of course I wish to be told if anything is not as nice as it can be. Let me taste the marmalade."

Miss Basden offered a spoon from the pot.

"It seems to me that it is very nice. Perhaps I am not a judge of marmalade. I do not care to eat it on bread with butter myself. One or the other is enough for me. But it seems to be very nice."

"Mother, don't water the boys' preserves," said Mr. Merry, nodding his head up and down. "Don't try to make things go further than they will go, you know. The game isn't worth the candle."

"I do not understand you, dear. There is never any extra water in preserves. They would not keep if they had water in them. There would not be any object in it. It would be less economical, not more."

"Oh, well, Mother, I don't know anything about the kitchen business and that. But if the marmalade is not right, let us have it right another time. That is all I mean."

"I do not think you know what you mean, dear."

"No, Mother, no; very likely I don't."

"The housekeeping is not your province, Mr. Merry," said Miss Basden. "You will have us coming and telling you how to teach Latin, if you are not careful."

"Ah, Miss Basden, ah, you saucy lady!" '

A source of amusement is the invariable curiosity of the minor characters about the central tragedy; this is dissembled by the dishonest, and frankly acknowledged by the more worthy.

'Our curiosity is neither morbid nor ordinary. It is the kind known as devouring.' (Evelyn Seymour, in *Daughters and Sons*.)

'We can't put gossip off until we return from London. It has a frail hold on life like all precious things.' (Julian Wake, in *Brothers and Sisters*.)

'I don't like things to pass me by, without my hearing about them. We are meant to be interested in what the Almighty ordains.' (Sarah Middleton, in *A Family and a Fortune*.)

The brilliance and wit of the dialogue have increased with each successive book. Even in the more conventional and easily detachable epigrams there are turns and rhythms which unmistakably show their author: 'Saying a thing of yourself does not mean that you like to hear other people say it. And they do say it differently.'

'Being cruel to be kind is just ordinary cruelty with an excuse made for it. And it is right that it should be more resented, as it is.'

The extraordinarily subtle humour of her finer writing would need illustration by a long, sustained passage, though it is suggested by such a passage as this from *More Women Than Men*, where Felix Bacon is talking to Josephine Napier about the staff of her school.

' "I hope they none of them presume upon their friendship?"

"I trust that they deal with me fully as a friend. I hardly understand that phrase, 'presume upon friendship'."

"I quite understand it. Shall we have a gossip about your staff?"

"No!" said Josephine. "When you have known me a little longer, you will know that my mistresses, in their presence and in their absence are safe with me. I hope I could say that about all my friends."

"I hoped you could not. But it is interesting that they would not be safe if we had the gossip. They must have treated you fully as a friend. I almost feel we have had it." '

It is not to be supposed that the characters in Miss Compton-Burnett's novels are only types, because they are easily classifiable. They are in fact very subtly differentiated. They are limited on the whole to certain broad categories, because the plot is to deal with certain kinds of happenings. Since the happenings come out of the people, that entails certain kinds of people. Happenings cannot come out of types, they must come out of real characters. The twelve tyrants, for example, all stand out distinct in the memory: though similarity of situation may sometimes cause them to speak alike, one could in nearly every case pick out the speech of one from that of all the others.

Critics who are unwilling to take the trouble that this very difficult writer requires, or who are not sensitive to subtleties of speech, complain that all her people talk alike. She herself has written in the *Conversation*: "However differently characters are conceived — and I have never conceived two in the same way — they tend to give a similar impression, if they are people of the same kind, produced by the same mind, and carried out by the same hand, and possibly one that is acquiring a habit.'

Each of her characters talks like the others in the sense that they all talk with maximum clarity and self-revelation, and in a polished bookish speech — in this they are all more alike than they are like any character by any other writer. But they have all been conceived with such clarity that with patience they are easily distinguishable. Moreover two practices of the author's which make her characters superficially more alike, in fact mark their difference. When one character tries to imitate another, who is a more brilliant conversationalist, we are at once aware of the imitation — this could not be the case unless both characters were very distinct in our minds. (Thus in *Brothers and Sisters*, Latimer imitates Julian; in *Men and Wives*, Kate imitates Rachel Hardisty.)

Her second device occurs in her later novels, and is an even greater *tour de force*. She brings out family resemblances, so that in *A Family and A Fortune*, the little boy, Aubrey, combines something of the peevishness of his maternal grandfather, Oliver Seaton, with more of the clear-headed fineness of his paternal uncle, Dudley Gaveston (whose manner of speech he also consciously imitates). Nevertheless all three characters remain entirely distinct in the reader's imagination, and Aubrey is one of the most moving child characters in fiction. This sort of achievement is perhaps unique — it is much more than mere technical virtuosity, it is real character creation.

Her treatment of children is particularly admirable. Children in fiction have been more sentimentalized, lied about and betrayed than any other class of being. The more intelligent the writer, the better he treats them. Henry James and Proust have written better about them than anyone. An author so unsentimental and intelligent as Miss Compton-Burnett might be expected either to leave them alone, or to deal with them perfectly, as she has done. Although her narrative takes place almost exclusively in the form of very highly developed conversation among remarkably articulate people, she has all the same managed to draw shy and even very young children brilliantly — and she knows, what most people forget, how extremely early the character is distinct. Nevill Sullivan in *Parents and Children* is only three, and a very definite character, with his own kind of independence and protective cunning.

There are few more triumphant revelations of the child mind in English literature than in the scenes in *Elders and Betters* where Julius and Dora Calderon practise their extraordinary private religion. Their prayer to their God, after the death of their aunt and the suicide of their mother is often quoted.

'O great and good and powerful god, Chung, grant that our life may not remain clouded, as it is at this present. And grant that someone may guide us in the manner of our mother, so that we may not wander without direction in the maze of life. For although we would have freedom, if it be thy will, yet would we be worthy of being our mother's children. And if there is danger of our inheriting the weaknesses of our mother and our aunt, thy late handmaids, guard us from them, O god, and grant that we may live to a ripe old age. For it would not be worth while to suffer the trials of childhood, if they were not to lead to fullness of days. And we pray thee to comfort our father and our brother and sister; and if they are in less need of comfort than beseems them, pardon them, O god, and lead them to know the elevation of true grief.'

Miss Compton-Burnett's novels are certainly of permanent value, though they may never be 'popular classics'. Her work continues to become increasingly attractive to serious students of literature. Many will find her style rebarbative on a first approach: all must find it difficult. Only repeated re-reading can extract all the treasure from her finest work; and it is hard to persuade people to give the attention to a major novelist that they are ready to squander on minor poetry. It does not seem too much, or nearly enough, to claim for her that, of all English novelists now writing she is the greatest and the most original artist.

INDEX

INDEX

INDEX

INDEX